CW00949799

F

This book is due for return on or before the last date shown below.

5-9-07
- 8 OCT 2015

6 JUN 2022

planet earth the future

Environmentalists and biologists, commentators and natural philosophers

IN CONVERSATION WITH

Fergus Beeley

Mary Colwell and Joanne Stevens

BOOKS

10 9 8 7 6 5 4 3 2 1

Published in 2006 by BBC Books, an imprint of Ebury Publishing

Ebury Publishing is a division of the Random House Group

The Random House Group Limited Reg. No. 954009

Addresses for companies within the Random House Group can be found at
www.randomhouse.co.uk

A CIP catalogue record for this book is available from the British Library
The Random House Group Limited makes every effort to ensure that the papers
used in our books are made from trees that have been legally sourced from
well-managed and credibly certified forests. Our paper procurement policy
can be found on www.randomhouse.co.uk

The paper this book is printed on is certified by the © 1996 Forest Stewardship Council
A.C. (FSC). It is ancient-forest friendly. The printer holds FSC chain of custody
SGS-COC-2061

Commissioning editor: Shirley Patton
Project editor: Rosamund Kidman Cox
Designer: Jo Ridgeway
Production controller: Peter Hunt

Printed and bound in Great Britain by
Butler & Tanner Ltd, Frome, England

Jacket photograph by
Rinie van Muers/Foto Natura/FLPA

ISBN-10: 0563 53905 4
ISBN-13: 9780563539056

FSC
Mixed Sources
Product group from well-managed
forests and other controlled sources

Cert no. SGS-COC-2061
www.fsc.org
© 1996 Forest Stewardship Council

Contents

Foreword

by Jonathon Porritt

'So what are you guys going to do when that elusive tipping point of yours actually tips – and everybody *really* starts getting it? It won't be long, you know, and then you'll all be out of a job!'

These words – from one of today's world-weariest and most cynical of media commentators – made me laugh out loud. The idea of being out of a job because the whole world is suddenly 'doing sustainability' is too delightful a prospect to dwell on for more than a few seconds. But the idea of that long-sought-after sustainability tipping point being imminent is certainly one to conjure with – even as the cataloguing of environmental doom and gloom grinds remorselessly on.

All those who have pitched in their twopence-worth to this wonderful project are all – in one way or another – speculating about such a tipping point. But you'll find no easy consensus. Indeed, what astonishes me today is to see how differently different people interpret the same base-line data about the cumulative impact of the human species on planet Earth's life-support systems. Some will force you with them down to the very depths of despair, while others optimistically offer up a reassuring 'window of time' still available to us to get things sorted.

No-one quite knows how wide a window that may be. We're now 35 years on since the UN Conference on the Environment and Human Development in Stockholm in 1972 first gave voice to the same broad analysis that you will find here. It goes almost without saying that not enough has been done to address that analysis since then; but a huge amount has been achieved, and many destructive trends have been slowed if not, as yet, reversed.

And while there are a few who suppose we've got another 35 years, responses to this planetary crisis are both diversifying and deepening *rapidly*. In contrast to where we were 35 years ago, we seem to be getting both more worldly *and* more spiritual about it. More worldly in that you will find here all sorts of ideas for engineering some kind of accommodation with contemporary economic and political orthodoxies, embracing the power of the market, celebrating technological innovation, working with the grain of 'homo economicus' rather than against it.

And more spiritual. This text powerfully reinforces an idea that was only dimly discernible 35 years ago: that the crisis we now face is as much one of the human spirit as of ecological collapse. If there is a tipping point just around the corner, it must surely lie in the gathering realization (to paraphrase Albert Einstein!) that we cannot fashion durable solutions to today's problems based on the kind of mindsets that gave rise to those problems in the first place.

In that regard, perhaps the biggest shift of all lies in the rediscovery of our *total* dependence on the Earth's natural systems and services. It may once have made sense to assert our dominance as a species by seeking to subjugate 'the rest of life on Earth', but as we made war on nature, so we made war on ourselves.

However optimistic or pessimistic they may feel, whether they're scientists or spiritual leaders, all those whose voices you will hear in this book and in the TV series *Planet Earth – The Future*, from which these quotes are taken, are saying the same thing: now is the time to step away from those childish but increasingly lethal fantasies.

It's not quite the same thing as a populist tipping point. But the combined weight of, on the one hand, nearly 50 years of authoritative scientific research revealing the intimate workings of the natural world, and on the other hand, of new (or rediscovered) philosophical insights about the unfolding of life on Earth over 4.5 billion years, is overwhelming. It's time for us to grow up, to become truly ourselves.

The Contributors

Dr Neville Ash, Head of Ecosystem Assessment for the United Nations Environment Programme World Conservation Monitoring Centre (UNEP-WCMC).

Sir David Attenborough, world-famous broadcaster, television presenter and commentator on the natural world.

Dr Mark Brownlow, one of the producers of *Planet Earth* for the BBC Natural History Unit.

James Connaughton, Senior Environmental and Natural Resources Advisor to the President of the United States.

Huw Cordey, one of the producers of *Planet Earth* for the BBC Natural History Unit.

Robert Costanza, Director of the Gund Institute for Ecological Economics at the University of Vermont, USA.

Ahmed Djoghlaf, Assistant Secretary General of the United Nations and Executive Secretary of the United Nations Convention on Biological Diversity.

Dr James A. Duke, leading medicinal-plant scientist.

Johan Eliasch, successful businessman who has used his profits to safeguard rainforest by purchasing it.

Alastair Fothergill, Series Producer of *Planet Earth* for the BBC Natural History Unit and director of *Earth*, the feature film.

John Hare, Chairman of the Wild Camel Protection Foundation.

Dr Chadden Hunter, world expert on the geladas of Ethiopia.

Tony Juniper, Executive Director of Friends of the Earth and Vice-Chair of Friends of the Earth International.

Jan Kees Vis, Chairman of the Roundtable on Sustainable Palm Oil.

Peyton Knight, Director of Environmental and Regulatory Affairs for the National Center for Public Policy Research, a US communications and research foundation dedicated to free-market solutions.

James P. Leape, Director General of WWF International.

Dr Thomas Lovejoy, distinguished tropical and conservation biologist and President of the Heinz Center in the US.

Dr James Lovelock, distinguished scientist and originator of the Gaia hypothesis.

Dr Barbara Maas, Chief Executive of Care for the Wild International.

Professor Wangari Muta Maathai, Kenya's Assistant Minister for the Environment and creator of the Green Belt Movement.

Richard Mabey, one of Britain's foremost writers and a leading commentator on nature and our relationship with it.

Dr Jeffrey A. McNeely, Chief Scientist for the IUCN – The World Conservation Union.

Nisar Malik, Chief Executive of Walkabout Films, a conservationist and an extreme-events organizer based in Pakistan.

Dr Tony Martin, world-expert on dolphins and whales, working for the British Antarctic Survey.

Robert, Lord May of Oxford, President of the Royal Society (2000-2005), Professor in the Department of Zoology, Oxford University, and at Imperial College, London, a Fellow of Merton College, Oxford, and previously Chief Scientific Adviser to the UK Government.

Dr Russell A. Mittermeier, President of Conservation International and prominent primatologist, herpetologist and conservationist.

Dr Craig Packer, world-expert on lions and Distinguished McKnight Professor in the Department of Ecology, Evolution & Behavior at the University of Minnesota.

Martin Palmer, Secretary General of the Alliance for Religions and Conservation, and Religious Adviser to WWF.

Dr Roger Payne, leading whale biologist and founder and President of the Ocean Alliance.

Dr Paul Pettitt, Senior Lecturer in Palaeolithic Archaeology at the University of Sheffield.

Jonathon Porritt, leading writer, broadcaster and commentator on sustainable development, and co-founder and Programme Director of Forum for the Future.

Sandra Postel, leading authority on international freshwater issues and Director of the Global Water Policy Project.

Adam Ravetch, award-winning film-maker specializing in the Arctic.

Dr M. Sanjayan, Lead Scientist for the US Nature Conservancy.

Clare Short MP, former Secretary of State for International Development (DFID).

Peter Smith, Roman Catholic Archbishop of Cardiff.

Dr Mark Stanley Price, Chief Executive of the Durrell Wildlife Conservation Trust and founder and Chair of the World Conservation Union's (IUCN) Reintroduction Specialist Group.

Dr Robert T. Watson, Chief Scientist at the World Bank in the Sustainable Development Network.

Dr Rowan Williams, Archbishop of Canterbury, Primate of All England and leader of the Anglican communion.

Professor E.O. Wilson, one of the world's most distinguished biologists and thinkers, Honorary Curator in Entomology at Harvard University, leading expert on ants and promoter of the concept of biodiversity and originator of the term biophilia.

What Extinction Crisis?

1

Many of the animals featured in *Planet Earth* are endangered, from the Amur leopard in Russia's Far East and the Bactrian camel in Outer Mongolia to the frogs of Central America. Does it really matter if some of them become extinct? Do some matter more than others? If we don't even know how many species there are on Earth, can we really have any idea of how many are threatened?

I don't think there's any denying that this is a crisis moment, and I don't think there's any denying that it's gotten worse in the last 30 years – that we have pushed steadily closer to the brink of disaster in many of the systems that support life on Earth.

We are now at the point where we have lost half of the world's forests, half of the world's wetlands, half of the world's grasslands. We are systematically eradicating many of the habitats that make up the world's ecosystems, and that cannot be a good thing for the animals who live there, or for the people who depend on them.

We do know that, of the species we've identified, we have perhaps one in four mammals and a third of all amphibians on the threatened list. So we know that we are progressively pushing more and more species to the edge of extinction, and we know that those species are the building blocks of the ecosystems that support life.

JAMES LEAPE

We used to have 1000 species go extinct every year. Now we are maybe losing between 15,000 and 60,000 species a year. When we discover a new species, it is a newspaper headline because it's something exceptional. But the rate of extinction is not exceptional – it's not in the newspapers – because it's business as usual.

We have just finalized a study conducted by 1300 experts from 95 countries, and the results are really terrifying. Never have human beings destroyed the beauty that is life on Earth as we have done for the last 50 years. So, yes, we are in a crisis moment.   **AHMED DJOGHLAF**

In human timescales, we tend to regard 10 or 20 or 30 years as quite a long time. And to that extent, those who've been hearing the call for action to avert a mass extinction of species think that it has been around for quite some time, nothing's really happened and therefore things probably aren't as bad as we thought.

But you have to remember that the timescales that biological systems are responding to are millions of years or at least hundreds of thousands of years long. And so the extinction that's taking place now and which has been going on for some hundreds of years and which is accelerating into the future – this is something that's happening in the mere blink of an eye in terms of the life of this planet. And so we do need to take a longer perspective than just a few years in terms of how serious this crisis is.

What I've understood from the data coming from countries worldwide and from the scientific community is that we now face an extinction episode on this planet comparable to that which marked the end of the dinosaurs about 65 million years ago. It's largely driven by habitat change, by the release of pollution into the environment, by global warming and by the exploitation of species directly, as well as by introductions of animals into lands where they're not native.

All these things are combining in a series of forces likely to lead, if we don't take action very soon, to the extinction of a large proportion of this Earth's species. There is still time to do something about that, but time is extremely short.   **TONY JUNIPER**

Well, biodiversity has been around for billions of years now, and it's changed over time, and it's had its moments of great crisis, like when the dinosaurs disappeared. But if you ignore those moments of crisis and just look at it over time, it's been an increasing curve. So we live today easily at the greatest moment for biodiversity on Earth. The great irony is that we are living at the optimum moment to date in the history of life on Earth, and rather than glorying in it and revelling in it, we're busily collectively destroying it. It's not to say there haven't been major advances in conservation in the last 20 years, but this is a race to the finish, and so far biodiversity is losing. **THOMAS LOVEJOY**

the great irony is that we are living at the optimum moment to date in the history of life on Earth, and rather than glorying in it and revelling in it, we're busily collectively destroying it

If you just lose one species, it's probably not going to have a big impact, at least nothing that you and I will recognize. But if we continue to lose loads and loads and loads of species, what we're actually saying is that the underlying fabric of nature is tearing. And that tearing will have huge repercussions for the well-being of people who live within that environment. Eventually you will get down to the point where you're not going to have water in the streams, you're not going to have forest cover, you're not going to have meat to fill your bellies, you're not going to be able to find fuel wood. That I think is the real crisis that people worry about. From an ethical or moral point of view, losing any single unique life form is a crisis, is something that I abhor. But for the vast majority of people who live on this planet, life may be blinking out all the time, but they don't know about it, nor will they know about it even if the rates increase. But eventually what's going to happen, and it has happened in some places, is that so many things will be lost that the whole fabric of nature will have been torn apart. And that will be noticeable. **M. SANJAYAN**

Human history has faced a continuous succession of crises. The species-extinction crisis that is so worrisome today may have been even worse at certain earlier times in history, at least for large animals. For example, 43 genera of large mammals became extinct within a few thousand years after the first people settled the western hemisphere about 15,000 years ago. As many as 2000 species of birds became extinct shortly after the Polynesians spread into the Pacific. So at certain moments in history, humans can have a massive impact, usually linked to new technology and an expanding population. Right now is one of those times when we're having a massive impact. We're expanding our numbers, we're expanding our economic use of resources, we're developing new technologies, and the rest of the species are suffering as a result. **JEFF MCNEELY**

yes, there is a crisis, but we are the endangered species more than anything else

A moment is a different measure in human existence than in biological existence. We're not in a crisis, at least not in the next ten years. In the next century? Probably we are going to be. But I think it's us that's in the crisis more than the living systems of the planet. It's impossible to disentangle the two, but if climate change goes on unabated, there will be massive changes in the ecology of the planet, many ecosystems will probably vanish altogether, but by no means the majority of them. Humans, though, are going to suffer very badly. The rising of the sea level, enormous human migrations out of areas where agriculture becomes very difficult. These are going to present profound problems for the human species.

In pockets way beyond our influence, life will go on, and if, as James Lovelock predicts, the crisis will in fact happen to such a degree that the human population is massively reduced and has to retreat to living in the Arctic, then obviously the rest of the planet will have a ball. And other kinds of ecosystem which are adapted to hot climates and rapid change will flourish. So I think one has to take a relativistic answer that, yes, there is a crisis, but we are the endangered species.   **RICHARD MABEY**

We are on the steepening curve of a wave, if birds and mammals and some of the sexier plants over the last century are typical. And there are four different lines of argument that see a further steepening of that curve over the next century. So, independent of our lack of knowledge of how many species there

we are on the breaking tip of what will be a sixth great wave in the extinction of life on Earth

actually are, we can see we are on the breaking tip of what will be a sixth great wave in the extinction of life on Earth, differing from the big five previous ones, which were caused by external environmental events, by being deliberately associated with our activities.   **ROBERT MAY**

The effect on the imagination is different from the effect on the body. From a human point of view, we would be most saddened by losses of creatures which have become totems for us – the great whales, the tiger. Every time I think about the tiger, I think about about probably the best known poem in the English language – Blake's *The Tyger* – which every child can recite, and every child understands what it means. 'Tyger! Tyger! burning bright, in the forest of the night.' And they know that it's not just dark forest, it's to do with the pulse of life – deep down, both in our imaginations and in the world outside. And if we lose these majestic creatures with their sense of power and ancestry, and their possibility of power over us sometimes, then we as well as the ecosystem are diminished by that. We lose a measure of our own significance or insignificance when some of these astonishing creatures go.

RICHARD MABEY

We've always been in crisis moments, for particular ecosystems, particular kinds of organisms, particular species. They've been going extinct right and left – 90 species of freshwater fishes from the rivers of

> if we tell our descendants that ... we're sorry we didn't pay attention, we're sorry we were so destructive, but we had to get on with life ... they are going to be peeved

Malaysia, as many as 80 or more plant species wiped out by deforestation on one mountain ridge in Ecuador. But the crisis that we face now is that the rate of extinction is accelerating and that it will reach biblical proportions within a few decades.

If you go back 450 million years and then come forward, when life is on the land, the diversity was relatively low. Then it picked up considerably, with all sorts of new niches being opened and filled, and then flight came along after 100 million years or so – insects – and then other more elaborate forms of life. And as this process unfolded – that is, life as a whole pushed harder, opened new realms, developed new specializations and became more complex and diverse – Earth was hit by a number of extinction events, of which five were catastrophic. And after each one of these, for example, the one that ended the Palaeozoic era and began the age of reptiles, and the one that 65 million years ago ended the age of reptiles, as we call it, and set the stage for the beginning of the age of mammals, these took out quite a large percentage of the species of plants and animals on the Earth, and it took 10 million years roughly for each one of these losses to be recovered by further evolution. Ten million years. And that's something to bear in mind, as we allow extinction to proceed to such horrendous levels in this present century. If we allow this to go on and do not try to slow it or halt it, then we will likely have lost as many as half of the species of plants and animals at the end of this century.

In a way it's rather comparable to the end of the age of reptiles 65 million years ago. And then if we tell our descendants that it's all right, we're sorry we didn't pay attention, we're sorry we were so destructive, but we had to get on with life – our year-by-year existence and our pleasure – and not to be concerned because evolution will restore it all in 10 million years, they are going to be peeved. **E.O. WILSON**

How important is it to discover new species?

Recently I finished a pretty careful study of the most abundant ant genus – a major group of ant species on Earth. I concentrated on the western hemisphere, where this genus, *Pheidole*, is located – it's the most ecologically important single genus. And when I finished my study, with over 5000 drawings, I had a total of 623 species accounted for, of which 344 were new to science – more than half. And now that genus amounts to about 20 per cent of all the known species of ants in the western hemisphere. It doesn't mean anything at all to discover a new species. Even birds, mammals, are coming in. Frogs are coming in – new species as the world is explored further. Something like one third of all amphibian species, including frogs known to science, have been discovered within the last 30 years. And this should make you ponder. It means that, particularly for the smallest organisms, we have virtually no knowledge at all in many critical areas of the world. We don't, for example, know enough about the nematode worms, the roundworms of the world, which make up four out of every five animals on the planet, to have any solid picture at all of the diversity of these important little animals that are everywhere in the world. **E.O. WILSON**

the crisis that we face now is that the rate of extinction is accelerating and that it will reach biblical proportions within a few decades

I was at a meeting in China a couple of years ago, where Chinese palaeontologists were announcing some new discoveries of dinosaurs. How utterly irrelevant. Who cares about dinosaurs? They've been extinct for 65 million years. But everybody in the audience was spellbound by the concept of these magnificent creatures having existed. Isn't it wonderful that such a diversity of these giant reptiles dominated our planet for hundreds of millions of years. For us to know that mysterious life forms are still lurking in places that we haven't yet looked and

for us to know that mysterious life forms are still lurking in places that we haven't yet looked and even in places we thought we knew well – to me, this is one of the things that makes biology so exciting

even in places we knew well – to me, this is one of the things that makes biology so exciting.

About 1.8 million species have been described, but we don't really know how many there are. Some scientists say 10 million, some say 15, some say 100. It could even be more than 100 million if we start looking at the bacteria in the oceans, on the ocean floor, in the soil. But if we focus just on the fewer than half a million creatures we know reasonably well – the mammals, birds, reptiles, amphibians, fish and plants – the things that are closer to us, easier to see, we can use them as indicators of what is happening to the others, the more obscure forms. And that gives us ample reason for serious concern. **JEFF MCNEELY**

We continue to find new species at the rate of about 15,000 a year. At the same time as we are discovering new species, we're also finding that because the records are mostly so scattered and not coordinated, many of the things we thought were new species have been discovered earlier somewhere else in some other museum.

So we're resolving those synonyms at a rate that the total addition of species each year is somewhat less than 15,000, though more than 10,000 a year. Very few of these are mammals or birds. Yes, maybe one or two new bird species and several mammals turn up a year, it's a tiny percentage. Nearly all of the 10,000 or more are invertebrates – mainly insects. **ROBERT MAY**

Just how many species are there?

The number of distinct species we've named and recorded is some-where in the range of 1.5 to 1.6 million. Even that number is uncertain, by about 10 per cent, because of the synonyms in different collections, which is astonishing. Yet we know every book in the Library of Congress, and they're all cross-catalogued. We know even less about what the total number of species may be. Conservative estimates would put it somewhere in the range of 5 to 10 million plants and animals. And so, if we took a really conservative estimate of only another 3 million to be discovered, twice as many as we currently know, and at the rate of 10,000, 15,000, 20,000 a year, that's several centuries to complete the catalogue. Even though there are ways we can speed up the cataloguing process, collecting the specimens in the first place is always going to remain the step that limits the rate at which we can do this.

ROBERT MAY

We know perhaps 6000 species of bacteria well enough to characterize them and give them a code or a name. There are that many species in a single handful of garden soil, all of those species virtually unknown. An estimate was recently made that, in one ton of soil, you can find 4 million species of bacteria – all of them, or virtually all, unknown. And you have to ask yourself, what are these species doing?

We know we depend on them for our own lives. But as we don't know what the vast majority of these creatures are, we are therefore at a considerable loss in making any firm scientific predictions about the fate of a pond, a river, a country, as we undergo these terrific changes that are occurring in climate, chemical environment, atmosphere.

We know enough to make a good estimate at least for most groups. For example, we have enough knowledge of birds, which have been quite thoroughly attended to for three centuries, of flowering plants, the same, where we believe we have knowledge of at least 80 per cent of the species, and to a lesser extent, frogs and other amphibians, and reptiles, to use these as sample groups, to determine approximately how many species there might

> in one ton of soil, you can find 4 million species of bacteria – all of them, or virtually all, unknown

be in other groups, species that we still have to discover, and then how many species are going extinct globally.

Using these model groups to make the estimate with is rather like taking a random sample of people in the south of Britain and finding that 1 per cent were dying of respiratory diseases every year. You could be pretty sure that that would be the case for other parts of Britain.

one of the great unknowns in science today is how much biological diversity there is on Earth

One of the great unknowns in science today is how much biological diversity there is on Earth. We have knowledge of and have put scientific names on maybe 1.8 million species of plants and animals, and micro-organisms to date. But that may represent, especially when we thrown in micro-organisms and small creatures – insects, small invertebrates – only about 10 per cent of all the species on Earth. We've only begun to explore this planet.   E.O. WILSON

Given that we don't know how many species there are, we certainly can't tell you how many species are going extinct each year.

Another way of putting our lack of knowledge is to say recent, very careful catalogues suggest that about one in five of all mammal species is under extinction threat, but only 3 per cent of fish, and by this assessment, only 6 in every 10,000 invertebrate species.

But if you put that a different way and ask what fraction of the species that have been evaluated for extinction threat, it's roughly the same for mammals – 23 per cent rather than 20. For fish, it's more than a quarter rather than 3 per cent. And for insects, it's a whopping more than two thirds of all species that have been evaluated for extinction threat. That says a lot about what we know, as distinct from what is. Given all those uncertainties, however, we can make a much more precise estimate of the rate of extinction if we assume that the well-known groups like birds and mammals and some groups of plants, and what's happened to them over the last century, are typical. And on that basis , about one bird or mammal species a year has gone extinct over the last century, from a group of species that are of the general order of 14,000 species.

That kind of rate, if it holds for the much larger number of insects and other creatures we don't know much about, is characteristic of the acceleration in extinction rates – above the 'background' [rate] in the half-billion sweep of the fossil record – that characterizes the big five mass extinction episodes like the one that did in the dinosaurs.

ROBERT MAY

Is it worth trying to save species from extinction?

There can be lots of economic reasons that someone could think of why you wouldn't want to put an extraordinary amount of money and effort into saving one animal that is on the edge of its range – the Amur leopard, for example, a small-range, critically endangered species.

My personal belief is that it is morally bankrupt to give up on things that we know are going extinct. It's one thing to talk about some animal dying, but quite another to talk about the end of life – the end of a unique life form that has taken millions and millions of years of evolution to bring to this point – that we have the ability to do something about. It's almost overwhelming to imagine what future generations will think of us if we don't even try.

So for me, when you talk about saving critically endangered species, the argument is nearly always a moral one. It comes from a moral belief that there is room on this planet for all of these things.   **M. SANJAYAN**

Another reason for keeping each single one is that every species is a masterpiece of evolution. Every time biologists settle down and study a particular beetle

every species is a masterpiece of evolution … a history that goes back on average hundreds of thousands to millions of years

or scorpion or butterfly or tree that might be rare and obscure, they find that they're looking at a history that goes back on average hundreds of thousands to millions of years. It's a product of the unsparing pressure of the environment, moulding that species by adaptation through natural selection. So it has an immensely complicated history.

When the American chestnut became largely extinct at the turn of the last century from an introduced fungus, that wiped out as much as a fifth or more of the American forest. The forest recovered without the chestnut, but at least seven moth species that lived in the tree went extinct with it.

Well, one of those might not seem very significant to the average person just reading about it, but each one of those moths contained enough genetic history and uniqueness to fill all volumes of the *Encyclopaedia Britannica* published since the 1700s and is a product of the history of this Earth that we should not erase carelessly.   E.O. **WILSON**

I think any extinction that is before its time matters. But if one was to pick two groups, it's at the very top and the very bottom – the anonymous organisms that keep the planet going and the big organisms that keep our souls and imaginations on fire.   **RICHARD MABEY**

On the one hand, there are real uncertainties about what will be the consequences for humanity of the great wave of extinctions that are going to unfold over the coming several centuries, well beyond the horizon of a single human lifetime. On the other hand, we need to be doing things now, and to do that, we have to engage many, many, many individuals, which involves appealing to the things that have emotional resonance. Anita Desai once said of the novelist V.S. Naipaul: 'He looks upon the world with an icy clarity beyond regret or hope.' Now, somehow, what we've got to do is balance this clarity of appreciation of the problem, but it has

in reality, you've got to work with what people can relate to – a mixture of heart and head

got to be *not* beyond regret and hope, and has to mobilize the emotions and the caring instincts of people. And so many of these things are a juxtaposition of trying to see the facts clearly but at the same time working with what will work. And hence I see it as entirely correct to be using the panda to represent the host of unknown insects which may be more important.

In the ideal world, given that we are going to lose species, I and others would like us to take a more analytic view when we try to evaluate what will preserve the greatest amount of independent evolutionary history of life on Earth, which would put much more emphasis on the invertebrates, less on the pretty plants and the charismatic megafauna. But in reality, you've got to work with what people can relate to – a mixture of heart and head.   **ROBERT MAY**

We should worry about extinctions at multiple levels. One has to be concerned about forever – about losing an entire species for all time. And that's a loss not only at a moral, spiritual level, but it's also a loss at a practical level. Each of these creatures plays a role in its ecosystem. If you think in terms of a brick wall, we are systematically knocking out bricks, and sooner or later the wall will collapse.   **JAMES P. LEAPE**

if you think in terms of a brick wall, we are systematically knocking out bricks, and sooner or later the wall will collapse

One estimate made in 1997 by economists and biologists was that the services provided to humanity – scot-free incidentally – by all those bugs and weeds and possibly seemingly disposable birds and the like was about $30 trillion. Now that's roughly equal to humanity's own productivity. But in holding water in the watersheds, filtering it and purifying it, pollination, cleansing the atmosphere, restoring soil and on and on through the other ecosystem services, we are getting an immense amount of value from wild creatures left alive, and the more of them there are, the better the job is done.

the kinds of benefits that ecosystems give us depend very much on the way those ecosystems function. And that in turn depends on having all the pieces, so that the ecosystems work as a well-oiled machine

It doesn't matter what the species is. It can be a bird of paradise. It might be one of my favourite animals, a Sumatran rhino, which is receiving hundreds of thousands of dollars of help to see it through and avoid extinction. But it also can be an obscure moth somewhere. Incidentally, we're not going to be spending a million dollars on this species and then a million dollars on that species, it's not that simple, and it's far better than that image projects.

Generally speaking, what we spot are places where there are large numbers of endangered species together. So to save one typically means you save them all, or a large part of them. This is the basis of the hotspot concept of conservation, and we now have several dozen of them identified for global conservation efforts.

Hotspots include the rainforests of West Africa, the mountain forest of East Africa, the great floral region of South Africa, the Mediterranean coast, the Western Ghats of India, the sagebrush of southwestern Australia, the transfrontier forest running down the mountain spine of South America, the Atlantic forest of eastern Brazil, and so on around the world.

These are areas with particular habitats within them that, if we save them all and if we could add some of the core areas of the remaining tropical forest wildernesses – the Congo, the Amazon and New Guinea – then we would save substantially more than half of the known species of plants and animals on Earth.   **E.O. WILSON**

As far as we can tell, the kinds of benefits that ecosystems give us depend very much on the way those ecosystems function. And that in turn depends on having all the pieces, so that the ecosystems work as a well-oiled machine.

If we start losing some of the pieces, like soil micro-organisms, we're going to lose the productivity of the soil and therefore the productivity of the crops upon which we depend. If we lose large carnivores, ecosystems become unbalanced and may suffer cascades of extinctions as a result.

Odd-looking deep-sea creatures like the dumbo octopus are part of ecosystems that need to function well if we are to be able to harvest the products that we need or benefit from the services the seas supply.

We know that the oceans are important sinks for carbon. We know that this process of carbon sequestration depends on the way that the systems function. Pieces have to fit together.

We don't know nearly enough to understand exactly the role that each of these species plays, but we do know that ecosystems are like finely tuned but robust machines. Ecosystems have redundancy within them, so that they can lose pieces but keep working. Species have gone extinct frequently in the past. But every time one of the main pieces goes extinct, the system functions in a different way.

JEFF MCNEELY

Whether one organism's extinction matters more than another's depends on your point of view. And I don't mean that in a casual way. Obviously, if some major groups of bacteria responsible for the rotting of animal and plant remains were to become extinct, or if some of the major plankton species which are a major sink for atmospheric cabon dixoide and whose oxygen output powers the marine foodchain were to become extinct, then that would have a much more profound influence upon the life of the planet than if the polar bear became extinct.   **RICHARD MABEY**

if some of the major plankton species … whose oxygen output powers the marine foodchain were to become extinct, then that would have a much more profound influence upon the life of the planet than if the polar bear became extinct

Is it worth spending a lot to save an endangered species?

I think our concentration on highly endangered species, especially very glamorous large endangered species, is a morally tricky one, but probably politically sound. I think that if we were to let go of those creatures that figure so much in people's love of nature, figure so much in the historical imagination, it would be very hard to mount a case for defending anything.

if we were to let go of those ceatures that figure so much in people's love of nature, figure so much in the historical imagination, it would be hard to mount a case for defending anything

It may be topsy-turvy. These are in some senses the surplus animals of the planet. They live on surplus, they're only there because everything below them produces an abundance of food. If you strip them off, things go on much as they were before. A few species survive in greater numbers because they're not eaten. So, they're not important in a functional sense. But I think that in the way that human beings view the ecosystem, view the planet, if we were not to defend the people's favourites, then the cause would be lost, because it would be hard to make a case for the defence of, say, the stinging nettle, which we need just as much.

RICHARD MABEY

You bet your life it's worth spending a lot. The expenditure of a few thousand, up to even a few million, dollars today, if it can bring a species through that has been on Earth for say a million years and has so much to give us, if we can keep it alive, in every sphere of human consciousness – aesthetic, scientific, relation to the environment – yeah, that's a very good investment. It's sure a better investment than conducting wars.   **E.O. WILSON**

it's sure a better investment than conducting wars

Biodiversity Matters

2

The term 'biodiversity' encompasses the huge variety of life. Why is it important? Are we conserving the right parts? *Planet Earth* featured many animals that viewers had not seen before or were low on the popularity scale, from strange deep-sea creatures to cave oddities. Are these any less important in the grander scheme of things than the familiar animals that we most associate with. Does it matter if we care about some species more than others?

Biodiversity is simply the totality of all variation in life forms. And in studying biodiversity, we approach it at three levels of biological organization. On the top level are the ecosystems, the shallow marine environment, the savannahs, the forest patches, the ponds. On the second level are the species of plants and animals and micro-organisms that make up each ecosystem. And the third level are the genes, the variety of genes that prescribe the species, that fill up and make up the ecosystems. Both the diversity in its own right and the way that biodiversity fits together to make the environment – a living environment – is the basis of modern biodiversity studies.   E.O. WILSON

In 1980 there were three of us, including Ed Wilson, who used the term biological diversity for the first time. I can remember having lunch with Ed and talking about biological diversity before then, but we didn't have a term for it – a collective term to refer to the variety of life on Earth. Then it emerged, and then there was a major conference on it. The Smithsonian was involved and the National Academy of Sciences, and the staff person at the academy who basically made it all happen, Walter Rosenberg, contracted it to biodiversity.

When we were first using it, at least in Ed's mind and my mind, we were just looking for a collective term for this species-rich community of life organized in various kinds of ways. Elliott Norse, who was the other person who used that term that year, brought it much closer to its current definition, which goes beyond that sort of diversity of species to talk about the diversity of ecosystems and even goes down to the genetic level and looks at the diversity genetically within species.

THOMAS LOVEJOY

Why is biodiversity so important?

I think we have to regard biodiversity as important because the planet regards it as important. The way life has evolved on Earth is by a massive profusion of creatures. It's happened continuously over thousands of millions of years – it's probably going on very slowly still. We need to understand and respect why that has happened. And it's quite plain that, on our planet, at least, the evolved solution to life was to invent as many organisms as possible to exploit the great variety of climates and geological niches, and to buffer against change.

these intricate solutions to 'how do you exist on the planet' are wonderful to me, not only aesthetically but ethically as well

We tend to think of change as being somehow inimical to natural systems. It's not. It's one of the great stimulants to the evolution of life. What the planet has produced as a kind of flush of cards is astonishing, and at any point where we diminish that diversity, or allow it to diminish, we are weakening the whole resilience of the system of life on Earth as well as stopping in its tracks these beautiful solutions to the challenge of living. How do you live hundreds of feet under water in an undersea volcano, in toxic gases and flowing sulphur at great temperatures? Life has invented a way of doing that, just as it invented birds that can fly almost above the level that human beings can survive without oxygen. These are wonderful things. These intricate solutions to 'how do you exist on the planet' are wonderful to me, not only aesthetically but ethically as well. So, biodiversity for me is a thing to be preserved, not just because of its astonishing beauty, but because it is what underpins life on Earth.   **RICHARD MABEY**

I believe what people should keep in mind when they think about biodiversity and the extinction crisis is how little we know about the world that is vanishing. I like to say that, when we evaluate biodiversity in the world, the creation, the living part of the environment, we should keep in mind three contributions that the rest of life makes to us, which should cause us to put a lot of value on each species individually. The first is that it supports our own lives. If we eliminated even more than a small part of the biodiversity, the world would become a lot less stable and we would be much more subject to crises – changes in the environment that would profoundly affect us. But more than that, we already can measure the ecosystem services that this conglomerate of species which make up the living part of the environment give us scot free. And that's approximately equal to the entire domestic product of the world, if you could put a dollar value on it.

Each species is a product of up to hundreds of thousands to millions of years of evolution. And each is exquisitely adapted to some part of the environment in which it lives and the way that it interrelates with other species. And that immense history hammered into its present form by generation after generation of pitiless environmental pressure

> what people should keep in mind when they think about biodiversity and the extinction crisis is how little we know about the world that is vanishing

> there's a lot of evidence that human beings are attracted to life forms through the diversity – that a lot of culture is grown from the emotional response we have to living forms in nature

is what we have before us today. It's an irreplaceable treasure. So we should value it for that reason. I like to say, too, that it has high value for its aesthetic importance to humanity. There's a lot of evidence that human beings are attracted to life forms through the diversity – that a lot of culture is grown from the emotional response we have to living forms in nature. And so there is a spiritual argument for watching after the creation. Biodiversity is the creation that should be of as much concern to everyone, including religious people, as it is to the scientists who study it.   **E.O. WILSON**

Biodiversity is important for two reasons. The first is the moral reason – the responsibility that stewardship puts upon us to protect the complexity of life of which we are part. The second is that, when you reduce biodiversity, which is a complicated way of saying when you exterminate species, you exterminate links in chains and produce very, very unpredictable and often disastrous consequences.

Take the frogs in Panama, for example. Their disappearance can have great consequences for the various creatures that feed upon them or the creatures that they themselves feed on. If they go, the insects proliferate. What happens then? Do some of those insects carry diseases? Every time you change the balance or, worse, eliminate a species, you risk ecological catastrophe.   **DAVID ATTENBOROUGH**

There probably is, overall, more biodiversity on Earth at this time than there ever was before, but it's declining rapidly to below lower levels. And in some respects, it's at the lowest that it's been in over 60 million years, and that is, of course, because of the mega fall of the big animals, the big birds. We've sheared off the big animals – in fact, our stone-age ancestors did a lot of that. And we have cut into the smaller animals. And now, for the first time in the history of life, we are doing in most of the plant life – trees, shrubs, annual plants and so on – in terms of pure diversity, numbers of species.

E.O. WILSON

There are three reasons one should worry about diminishing biological diversity. One of them I would call narrowly utilitarian. You could say other species are the raw stuff of tomorrow's biotech revolution. Personally I don't find that very compelling. Quite apart from anything else, I think as we understand the molecular machinery of life, we'll build things from the bottom up. The second is more broadly utilitarian but still has us at the centre, and it says we count on the services that ecosystems deliver for many of the things we take for granted in life, and in an attempt to estimate the economic value of ecosystem services, puts their worth more than conventional global GDP. But I suspect we could probably be clever enough to live in a biologically impoverished world – the world of the cult movie *Blade Runner*. Which brings us to the third reason, which is a straight ethical reason: the responsibilities of stewardship to hand on a world not greatly biologically impoverished from the one we inherited. But that is a stronger argument from the luxury of the developed world than if you're struggling to make a living and feed six kids in the developing world.

ROBERT MAY

Where is most biodiversity found?

Diversity varies across the planet, and there's a broad generalization that says things are more diverse in tropical regions than they are at the poles. One among many unfortunate consequences of that is that the places where the greatest number of species are threatened tend to be the places where people can least afford to do something the places where the greatest number of species are threatened tend to be the places where people can least afford to do something about it about it – a strong negative correlation between per capita wealth and per capita biodiversity, if you like.   **ROBERT MAY**

> there are plenty of places on the planet that are not biodiverse, which have relatively few numbers of species but are hugely important for maintaining life … Think about mangroves

The whole focus on biodiversity and the conservation movement's grasping at the biodiversity straw have been a little misguided. We felt, because we're scientists, that what wows us – the diversity of life on Earth – should wow ordinary people. And it turns out it doesn't.

There are plenty of places on the planet that are not biodiverse, which have relatively few numbers of species but are hugely important for maintaining life on this planet, both human and non-human life. Think about mangroves. Now we know mangroves are imperilled and play a really important role in lots of people's lives. They are nurseries for fisheries. They provide fuel wood. Yet mangroves have exceedingly poor biodiversity, compared to, say, a tropical rainforest.

So biodiversity – as measured by number of species – is important, but we should never make the mistake to think that, just because a place has more diversity than another, it is automatically more important than another.   **M. SANJAYAN**

The idea of life coming out of barrenness has always been a powerful one for me. I think that it's a symptom of our rather narrow thinking about what constitutes fertility that we even use words like 'desert'. When you examine an ecosystem like a desert, which appears to be lifeless, you immediately begin to discover the great intricacy of parsimonious life that has worked out a way of living in these extreme conditions. And when that is demonstrated a hundredfold in that magnificent moment when rain falls on a desert and the dormant seeds suddenly erupt into life, for me it is not only profoundly beautiful but it's a slap in the face for everybody who believes that life depends, let's say, at one extreme, on masses of artificial fertilizer.

We have such a narrow vision of what fertility is about. We think in terms of deep soil. Most of the planet manages to get by on substrates we wouldn't even recognize as soil, and that moment the dormant seeds in a desert are brought into this astonishing flowering is to me a symbol of the fact that, even in the most deprived conditions, life manages to be triumphant.

It is a caution to us in our casual use of the words, not just 'desert', but 'wasteland'. No land is wasted if organisms make a livelihood there.

RICHARD MABEY

Do we need every single species?

When you start decreasing the numbers of species, especially in an environment which is adapted to a high level of diversity, you start reducing the stability of the area. The living environment becomes less able to take environmental shocks. It becomes less productive. That is the conclusion of a lot of work in ecology in the last 20 years, in theory and also in field experimentation. That's just the start. We know that wild environments and all those species together interlock in specializations to keep the ecosystem humming, so to speak.   E.O. WILSON

You take an animal like the snow leopard. There's no reason for it not to persist. There's no reason why it should become extinct. And that's the tragedy of it. You know the question really isn't, why does the snow leopard matter, why is it important? I can come up with reasons why it's important. It can provide some tourism dollars, it can regulate animals — herbivores — that might be competitors to people who are grazing their own animals and so on. The question is, does the snow leopard really have to disappear from the landscapes of India or Bhutan or Tibet for people to have a better life? My feeling is *no*. The truth of the matter is, if the snow leopard disappeared from the Himalayas, it's not going to make poor people rich all of a sudden. They'll still be poor, except now they won't even have the snow leopard.

M. SANJAYAN

The pygmy hog lives in these very tall grasslands, and while the eye is caught by large animals crashing their way through, there's another community on the grassland floor which is running around in the spaces between. The pygmy hog is undoubtedly helped by the effects of those large animals making the place open, and then new grasses sprout up, and the pygmy hog feeds on those. Now the pygmy hog is probably part of a large food chain of other predators. Tigers undoubtedly eat them, as well as pythons, small carnivores such as leopard cats, and birds of prey. So they're contributing to a whole smaller subset of food chains and webs and so on – much less obvious but still going on. And I would argue that, if you lose that pygmy hog, if you lose that bite-sized pig, a lot of other things may suffer as well.

MARK STANLEY PRICE

The wild camel has an immune system which is possibly stronger than any other mammal's. That's an extraordinary fact. Further south of the Gobi 'A', a Mongolian reserve in China, lies what used to be the Chinese nuclear-test area, which is where our foundation has helped to set up with the Chinese one of the largest nature reserves in the world. The Chinese exploded 43 atmospheric nuclear devices, and the wild camel survived. It hasn't got three humps or five legs or whatever. Is this to do with the immune system? In Mongolia, there's fresh water, but you get the wolves. In the Chinese reserve, there is no fresh water. There's salt water, which is why China chose the area as a nuclear test site. And the wild Bactrian camel will drink salt water that the domestic Bactrian camel will not touch, even though it's thirsty. So when we went into the reserve, we had to carry our own water for the camels. And yet the wild camels are managing to drink this water. Now that's extraordinary.

The 3 per cent base genetic difference with the domestic Bactrian is very important because the possibility is that it could be a separate species. Now, that hasn't been confirmed, but it's a possibility. But the point which is highly significant is that this animal can do something which the domestic Bactrian camel cannot do, and that's survive on this salt water. It's adapted to drinking the salt water because humans have pushed it into this harsh environment where there is only salt water, and yet it's managed to survive there. Surely it must be worth saving a creature with so many of these wonderful characteristics? **JOHN HARE**

Domestic Bactrian camels have a rather narrow genetic base. So suppose something like mad-camel disease comes along and hits the domesticated Bactrian camels. The wild Bactrian camels may well have genetic adaptations that would enable crossbreeds between wild and domestic individuals to resist that disease.

Numerous species of camels once roamed North America. When humans first arrived there, they found camels, horses and other large mammals. They drove many of them to extinction, leaving few domestic animals other than llamas, dogs, guinea pigs and

we can't predict the future, but the more we're able to keep our options open, the better our chances are likely to be for adapting to whatever challenges the future new world may bring

turkeys. So when the Conquistadors followed Christopher Columbus, the native American cultures were vulnerable to these European invaders, who had more domestic animals and therefore more options open to them to adapt to what was a 'new world'. We can't predict the future, but the more we're able to keep our options open, the better our chances are likely to be for adapting to whatever challenges the future new world may bring.   JEFF MCNEELY

The megafauna and megaflora – the rhinoceroses and the great sequoias and so on – have our attention and our affection, but in the long term, they are of no greater importance to humanity than are the bugs and the weeds – the little species. It's all a matter of awareness of what is there in nature and what is happening in nature and through nature to us by the rise and fall of floras and faunas.

My concern is the great indifference that most people have towards the species of creatures that they never notice or dismiss as bugs and weeds, and that's where the bulk of life on Earth exists. And when you magnify one of these organisms to human size, you approach it as an independent, highly complicated entity, you see it as the equal of a large mammal. I think that if we could magnify a beetle to be as large as a rhinoceros, that beetle in many ways would be more interesting than a rhinoceros.

my concern is the great indifference that most people have towards the species of creatures that they never notice or dismiss as bugs and weeds, and that's where the bulk of life on Earth exists

It's size alone that captures our attention, and that's a crudity of the psychological bias of human attention, which won't be there forever, certainly not in our descendants, who will come to appreciate every one of those little bugs and weeds on Planet Earth. They'll regret our having lost any one of them, for any number of reasons, particularly where there was no need to lose them.

E.O. WILSON

Why bother with the rare species when you've got so many common ones? The point is, if you look at the distribution and the numbers of species, a lot are rare. Relatively few are common. So if you lose the rare ones, you lose a very high percentage of your total biodiversity. And if you can't protect the rare today, you're not going to protect the common tomorrow. You get cascade effects, or you get populations falling below levels from which they can never recover. So I think we have to be very careful. There can be no complacency about allowing anything, really, to go extinct. The short-term ecological impacts may not be evident, but you are basically grinding ecosystems down to dysfunction, and then we shall all suffer. **MARK STANLEY PRICE**

The organisms that matter perhaps most of all in all these equations are the plants. Many of them are unglamorous, hard-working, abundant species but, of course, without them there would be no way in which the energy of the sun was translated into available energy for all other organisms.

photosynthesis, that chemical miracle by which light, water and air are transmuted into living matter, is the most crucial process in the whole biological world

Plants are the primary life on the planet. Everything else depends upon them. If one thinks of ecosystems as pyramids, plants are at the very bottom and yet are the most profoundly important. And if they were pulled away, obviously there would be nothing for anything to live on.

Photosynthesis, that chemical miracle by which light, water and air are transmuted into living matter, is the most crucial process in the whole biological world. And plants are a wonderful kingdom in their own right, full of the same ingenuity and inventiveness that you find in higher organisms. If one was to think in planetary terms rather than human terms, it is that underpinning of the whole of creation that is the vital importance of plants.

We have the same attraction towards the familiar and the glamorous in the plant world as we do in the animal world. We love bluebells for their smell and the way they symbolize an English woodland in spring. We love the glamour and exotic allure of orchids from the rainforest and their extraordinary ability to live on air – unearthly plants both in their biology and in the way they look. And yet underneath all these, I mean both literally and metaphorically, are the little humdrum plants: the mosses that are often the first things to move in to colonize bare rock, the parasitic plants that help decompose half-dead wood, the plants that have coevolved with animals – the grasses. Large areas of the planet are covered by grasses, which evolved along with herbivores. And these beautiful partnerships you see in all kinds of other parts of the ecosystem.

Research on the canopy is, I think, now the most exciting field of ecology – showing just to what extent plants live in really quite unexpected relationships, one with another and with other creatures. One of the most fascinating early discoveries which canopy scientists found was a phenomenon which completely contradicted the idea of the constant battles that early thinkers had about the jungle, as it was called then. They discovered that, at the growing tips of rainforest trees, the twigs weren't lashing each other and competing for light, they were actually moving away from each other, allowing growing space. They gave this phenomenon the rather touching and not terribly scientific name – crown shyness – though it looks more like crown respect than shyness to me. And this is symbolic of the whole way in which canopy plants work one with another.

sure, it's tough out there, but there are more solutions, which are made by accommodation, by partnership, by symbiosis, by association, than there are by outright violent struggle

You need to think about evolution at an ecosystem level to make sense of it, because rainforests partially survive by having enormous numbers of species in small areas. It's not like the English woods where you have loads of oaks or loads of beech all together. Eight hundred different species in a hectare is possible, and that is necessary to maintain each species' survival against blights and diseases and parasites and suchlike.

It would be a complicated mathematical trick that I couldn't do to show how that could be translated into the phenomenon of crown shyness, but I'm sure that's the purpose it serves. It also seems to me a great corrective to some of the glib Victorian assumptions we have about the way that life is lived in the wild – the struggle for survival. Sure, it's tough out there, but there are more solutions, which are made by accommodation, by partnership, by symbiosis, by association, than there are by outright violent struggle, and I think this is a good thing for us to understand.

RICHARD MABEY

If you look at the history of medicine, a large part of it is based on fairly frequent serendipitous discoveries of how biological systems work in other species, which then can be applied to our own well-being. And so in one sense, beyond the ecosystem services and all the goods that we can get from the natural world, it's really a living library, and it's just ridiculous to burn the books.

THOMAS LOVEJOY

beyond the ecosystem services and all the goods that we can get from the natural world, it's really a living library, and it's just ridiculous to burn the books

The role of plant-based medicines in conventional medicine is still very high. I don't know the exact figure, but I've certainly seen figures of between 20 and 40 per cent of all prescription medicines having a wild plant product somewhere in their ancestry, but it may be as remote as the shape of the molecule in the plant giving scientists the idea for the eventual drug. Prozac in that sense has one or two plant ancestors.

Many plants are still gathered for making medicines. One knows very well the damage the illegal derivatives of the opium poppy does, but opium poppies still make morphine and codeine and diamorphine and a host of other alkaloids. And the nightshade family, which is so productive of fantastically interesting plants and chemicals like tomato and potato, also produces hyoscene and hyoscyamine, which are used in the treatment of gut disorders and eye disorders. And, of course, many chemicals come directly from plants. Penicillin is a fungus. Aspirin no longer comes from plants, but it was invented from a distillate of willow bark and was named after meadowsweet [*Spiraea*], which also contains salicylic acid.   **RICHARD MABEY**

There is a very wide range of practical reasons why we need to conserve this planet's biodiversity. For a start, all of our food ultimately derives from biological systems. So do a lot of our medicines. A lot of our industrial products are based upon chemicals that we've taken from nature. Biodiversity is very much part, therefore, of the global economy, very much part of our well-being. We also need to face the reality that this is the only planet we know which supports life, and to understand it better surely is the priority that we must have as the species that thinks and which does science on this planet. Surely it's our responsibility to document carefully, to understand and husband this incredible unique planetary resource. But for me, in the end, the reason why we shouldn't lose any more species is moral. We didn't create life. We've got no means to put it back. Therefore we don't have the right to destroy it.

TONY JUNIPER

> in the end, the reason why we shouldn't lose any more species is moral. We didn't create life. We've got no means to put it back. Therefore we don't have the right to destroy it

I don't think there's a single reason of an economic kind that compels us to preserve biological diversity, but insofar as there are reasons, one says: 'We want to preserve this gene pool because maybe we can use it' – very human centred. Maybe we can be clever enough to just understand the molecules ourselves.

The second says: 'We depend on the services ecosystems give – pollinating, cleaning water – and as we reduce the number of species, we can't be sure they will continue to deliver those services.' Maybe we could be clever enough to live in an impoverished world.

The third reason is a straight ethical reason that says: 'We have a responsibility of stewardship,' and how strong that is depends on the luxury you have to enjoy it.   **ROBERT MAY**

Why do we care more about the glamorous species and ignore the rest?

If I was cynical, I might say that it's simply because they're given more media attention. I mean they're the celebs of the planetary ecosystem. One could go beyond that and say that the bigger an animal is, the more closely perhaps we can, in some way, get to grips with it and understand it. The smaller the component of the system and perhaps the superficially simpler the lifestyle, the more alien it often seems to us.

And yet if one was again to move away from purely human-centred standards of importance and say what are the important organisms for the continuation of life on the planet, tigers and elephants don't figure in it. They could be swept away by Gaia tomorrow, and the planet would still chug on.

If there was a planet-wide failure in plankton or in the anonymous and really extremely unglamorous mycorrhizal fungi that are are necessary for trees to grow, then the planet would collapse. These don't get television documentaries made about them, and they don't

> if there was a
> planet-wide failure
> in plankton or in
> the anonymous
> and really extremely
> unglamorous
> mycorrhizal fungi
> that are necessary
> for trees to grow,
> then the planet
> would collapse

you're not talking seriously about conservation until you include bacteria

figure yet in people's sense of being truly part of the natural world. Yet they are the vitally important building blocks, and they too need to be given respect.

An American ecologist friend once said that you're not talking seriously about conservation until you include bacteria. And I think we have to, if we're serious, move down the scale and consider these lowly organisms as being every bit as important as the big glamorous ones.

RICHARD MABEY

It is certainly true that in any given ecosystem there are some species of extraordinary importance to the health of that ecosystem. This is true of elephants, for example. Something like two thirds of the tree species in western Africa germinate only when processed through an elephant – an elephant eating the seed and excreting it in the forest. And elephants knock down trees; they clear open habitat where other species can thrive.

So there are some species in almost every ecosystem that are of particular importance. But it's also true that every species has a role.

JAMES LEAPE

The Threats and the Threatened

3

Many of the stars of *Planet Earth* are under increasing pressure – including Amazon river dolphins, Ethiopia's Walia ibex, the polar bear and the amphibians of Central America. And what endangers them endangers many other species and the habitats they are integral parts of. Here are some specific thoughts on some very specific representatives of a very unspecific, world-wide problem.

Conservation biologists and ecologists have a pretty good handle on what's causing extinction of ecosystems and of species. And it can be summarized with the acronym HIPPO. The first letter represents the most important factor and you go on down in order, although all of them are important.

H stands for habitat destruction, in the broadest sense, and we are unbelievably good at that. But that also includes the spectre of climate change, which we now see as one of the great destroyers of nature over the twenty-first century.

I is for invasive species. These are the introduced alien species which, all around the world, are spreading faster and faster and which push out and destroy native species. But they also include disease organisms. These are simply invasive species coming from different parts of the world, where they evolve or have been in place for a long time and sweep around and assault not only the human species, but also a lot of the natural species.

The first P of HIPPO stands for pollution, And let me give one example: 80 per cent of the rivers in China are now so polluted that they are unable to support any fish of any kind, and that indicates a probably horrendous amount of extinction of species in the river systems of China.

The second P is for overpopulation. That's a root cause.

And O is overexploitation. That's hunting and fishing species out of existence. And that's quite common, although it has not yet been of a magnitude as the other agents of destruction.   E.O. WILSON

The Amazon river dolphins

A week ago today, I was sitting on a raft in the Amazon wearing little more than a pair of shorts. It was a lovely time of year because many of the boto river dolphins that we've known for a decade or more were giving birth. But, unfortunately, at the same time we were increasingly discovering that large numbers of botos were being killed deliberately for fish bait. We're losing animals we've known for a long time, which of course is very distressing.

They're being killed because there's a new fishery for a type of catfish which hasn't been eaten in the Brazilian Amazon historically but for which a market has opened up in Colombia. This catfish eats dead meat, so botos are being killed. And it's because the Colombians have effectively fished out this species of fish.

We hardly noticed an effect at all in the first couple of years, but now it's very obvious. We're losing marked animals with regularity, and we hear that many of the villagers up and down the river are engaging in this practice. We're now trying to find out how many botos are being killed every year to provide the bait.

We often find wounded animals that have been harpooned. We've found some that have had rope tied around their tail, and I think what's happening is that they're being caught and then held as live bait until such time that they're needed for the fishery, and then they're killed.

It is pretty distressing and I think that what we're seeing is just the tip of the iceberg. I've been working out there now for 12 years, and originally we thought these animals were almost immortal. They seemed to be going on forever and ever. Each year we marked new dolphins, and those animals were seen day after day, week after week, year after year. But in the last few years, we've noticed that animals which were being seen very regularly have suddenly disappeared. Now, of course, they could all have suddenly moved away to Colombia or Ecuador or somewhere, but I think that's extremely unlikely. So I think the population is almost certainly declining now.

It makes me feel very sad. I'm a biologist, and I try to be as dispassionate as I can, but the fact is, we're following the lives of individual animals. You do get to know them very closely. Last week I saw one give birth. It was only for the second time in my life, and of course that stirs real emotions inside you. You try to stay very professional about it, but this is a new life being created, and at the same time, a few kilometres away, there are people taking those same lives and, in some cases, taking the lives of animals that I've known intimately for many years. So it is intensely sad and, of course, worrying from a broader perspective, the perspective of the population. **TONY MARTIN**

If you look at what the people along the Amazon depend upon as their main source of protein, it's fish. The Amazon river dolphins are top predators, like the caymans, and are part of the food chain with the hundreds of species of fish that live in the Amazon and upon which the local people depend. By sharing an ecosystem with the Amazon dolphins, people are part of a more productive ecosystem, and one that is better able to adapt to the changing conditions that certainly are

the more that we're able to maintain this diversity in the Amazon, the better the chances local people have of adapting to new conditions

the threats and the threatened 45

coming to the Amazon today. So the more that we're able to maintain this diversity in the Amazon, the better the chances local people have of adapting to new conditions. **JEFF MCNEELY**

Amazon river dolphins are unique among the river dolphins in that they are still relatively numerous. In all of the other places in the world where dolphins live in rivers, they're in big trouble. The extreme case is the one in China – the Baiji, which lives in the Yangtze; it maybe extinct as we talk and almost certainly will become extinct during our lifetimes.

In the Indus, which is reduced to a trickle at some times of year because the water is taken away for irrigation, there's a dolphin that's down to little more than a thousand individuals. The Ganges has another dolphin that's similarly in dire trouble. The fact is that humans and river dolphins don't mix. They're all after the same resources, water and fish, and it's inevitable that the dolphins come off second best.

I think botos are doing relatively well simply because there hasn't been the human pressure on them that there has been on the Asian dolphins. The Amazon is a very big place. There's a burgeoning human population there, but as yet humans haven't managed, for example, to denude the forest the way they have around the Yangtze.

The boto, just like the Baiji in China, is very much dependent on the rainforest. It goes into the flooded forest during the high-water season.

the fact is that humans and river dolphins don't mix. They're all after the same resources, water and fish, and it's inevitable that the dolphins come off second best

The Baiji used to do that as well, but there's now no forest left for it to fish in. The boto still has rainforest, but it does seem to be a matter of time. What we're seeing at the moment is a relatively rosy picture, but as every dam is constructed in Brazil and the Amazon, as more and more water is taken away for drinking and for irrigation, so of course there is less for the dolphins.

For centuries botos have been held in great esteem. There's a mythology that's been built up around them, and that's protected them. They're considered to be humans that have come back after death. But for some reason, certainly in the last decade, probably in the last five years, much of that mythology has disappeared in some communities.

I was talking to some villagers last week where some people in the community are killing dolphins, and they are very, very scared because they think there's going to be retribution as a result of that. But it's clear that the mythology is slowly breaking down, and I just can't see it being restored. That universal fear of doing harm to dolphins seems to have gone forever.

> dolphins are some of the most obvious of the larger predators, and because of that, they're easy to use as an indicator of the health of the whole ecosystem

Botos matter because they are an integral part of our world, and I think they have as much right to live here as we do. Do we have the right to modify the environment so greatly that they're unable to survive? They've been here for millions of years, and they've adapted to an environment that did not have humans in it. And then in the last century, with technology – particularly monofilament gill nets – they've suddenly been faced with dangers that they're not adapted to. They're an indicator of what we're doing to the Amazon rainforest as a whole.

If they disappear, the Amazon will, of course, continue. It is an area of such rich biodiversity, and dolphins are just a small part of that. The number of fish species, for example, is just mind-boggling, and there are many aquatic predators there other than dolphins. But dolphins are some of the most obvious of the larger predators, and because of that, they're easy to use as an indicator of the health of the whole ecosystem. The flooded forest is very vulnerable to man-made changes, and river dolphins as a whole and botos in particular need it. So, if the flooded forest is badly damaged, they will be among the first to show us what's going on.

Among the 80-odd species of cetaceans in the world – whales, dolphins and porpoises – there's only a very small number isolated in fresh water and adapted to this particular environment. These true river dolphins have evolved uniquely specialized features to allow them to live within the tangled rainforest. For example, they're able to turn their heads, unlike marine dolphins. They can even swim backwards, unlike marine dolphins. They have very long forceps-like beaks to be able to pick up fish.

In the Asian continent, the Indus dolphin and the Ganges dolphin are effectively blind. They find their way around with sound. They see with sound. They've lost the ability to use their eyes because they're effectively living in milky coffee. There's no point in having vision. So they've become very specialized. They've painted themselves into a corner, and now humans have come along and made this environment almost uninhabitable.

You're going along in your boat, and you have the dolphin just a few metres away. Normally they'll come to the surface every 30 or 60 seconds, then they suddenly disappear, and you wonder where they've gone. And then you'll hear this little 'puff' coming out of the dense forest, and you realize that they've just swum through the trees into a lake 100 or 200 metres inside.

What they're doing in there is exploiting fish in a way that they can't do for the rest of the year, when water levels are lower. And this is one of the characteristics that make river dolphins so special. They have the ability to go into the flooded forest, in water maybe only a metre or two metres deep, something that a marine dolphin would never attempt.

Those whales, dolphins and porpoises that cannot get away from humans are the ones in deepest trouble. River dolphins are the extreme examples. Similarly, coastal dolphins are in much more trouble than the oceanic ones. Oceanic dolphins and whales can get away. We did our damnedest to remove the blue whale from the planet, over many, many decades. We killed hundreds of thousands of them. But blue whales are still there, simply by virtue of the fact that some could get away – could live in the middle of the ocean and escape encounters with whalers. That cannot happen in a coastal or riverine environment.

TONY MARTIN

The iconic ibex

The Simien Mountains in Ethiopia is a magical place. It's somewhere you do not expect. Many people's images of Ethiopia are desert, famine. And here is this plateau rising up and surrounded by desert, an almost Shangri-La of cascading waterfalls and bubbling clouds and animals that you will never see anywhere else, big iconic animals like Walia ibex with horns sweeping back over their backs.

The landscape is incredibly dramatic. It's a mountain range created by erosion, not your typical mountain-range look, built up by geology. These mountains are carved away, and you get the most incredible shapes – eroded pinnacles, spikes and jagged crevices – and then these amazing animals that you will not see anywhere else, dotted around this incredible landscape. I was there for over a year studying gelada baboons before I ever saw a Walia. In Ethiopia you see their huge horns on emblems, and they're talked about religiously among the Ethiopians. They're very shy, and the first time that you see a Walia ibex – this silhouette with these magnificent big curved horns over its head – it's a very moving moment.

The Walia ibex has very sweet meat. Many highlanders rave about the taste. It was always a prize trophy animal to kill and to eat. And, in a place where humans are living on the edge, in terms of altitude and survival, being able to kill and eat a Walia was something that they saw as a right – a natural resource, to be harvested. And the Walia ibex horns are incredibly strong and prized ornaments, made into cups and decorations. And so to go into a place like Ethiopia and talk about not taking a resource that they've been utilizing for centuries involves a very difficult process of understanding.

> here is this plateau rising up and surrounded by desert, an almost Shangri-La of cascading waterfalls and bubbling clouds and animals that you will never see anywhere else

There's evidence that Walia ibex were once widespread throughout Ethiopia. If you go into small churches, there are paintings of them. If you go down to ancient ruins in the desert, they have engravings of Walia ibex, which would have been seen locally. It's only been with the warfare in the last century – the Italian invasion and then a big civil war – that the Walia ibex became favourite food for soldiers. The Simien Mountains saw a huge amount of fighting through the 1970s and 1980s, and in that period, the easiest food for a very cold soldier, lost in these mountains, would have been to take a shot at one of the Walia ibex on the cliffs. And so we saw the numbers decimated only in the last few decades, primarily a result of warfare. Ethiopia got flooded with AK47s, and when you have a growing population, a war and a country full of weapons, the Walia ibex is on the frontline.

the Walia ibex is such an important creature in Ethiopian culture and history and iconography that it's hard to put a price on what it would be like not to have this animal

The Walia ibex is such an important creature in Ethiopian culture and history and iconography that it's hard to put a price on what it would be like not to have this animal. Sixty million Ethiopians will never have seen a Walia ibex, because they're only found on this little section of cliff, but every single schoolchild in Ethiopia would be able to draw one. People use phrases about being as strong as a Walia ibex. If you talk to someone you work with in the field about them being as agile as a Walia ibex, they have this glowing look on their face. It is such a compliment.

When they got down to the last 150 Walia ibex, it really was the beginning of conservation generated from within Ethiopia. It was when Ethiopians themselves started turning around saying, 'Hang on. This animal is so iconic to our culture, to our nation. We put it on flags.' And so since then, in the last, say, 10 or 15 years, we've seen the number of Walia ibex come back from about 150 to 600. And that's one of the best good news stories that I've heard in African conservation.

Since it's been protected and the laws have become so strict on poaching, it's actually been able to spread back. But there aren't that many cliffs, and when you have farmland at the bottom of your cliffs and farmland at the top, there really is very little room for these Walia to spread into. And for the population to go through such a bottleneck, the genetic diversity is not very rich.

The one thing the Walia has going for it is the habitat that it lives in, these sheer, sheer cliffs. There are very few animals in the world that could live on precipices like the Walia can. And so it has a little niche that it can cling to, and as long as it's not shot, it should be OK within that little area. But it's such a fragile situation – 600 animals for a large mammal is nothing. And when you have no other habitats to spread into, no other populations to interbreed with, no Walia ibex in captivity, you'd better be sure that you can protect that one last piece of cliff that they have.

Ethiopians themselves started turning around saying, 'Hang on. This animal is so iconic to our culture, to our nation. We put it on flags.' And so since then, in the last, say, 10 or 15 years, we've seen the number of Walia ibex come back from about 150 to 600. And that's one of the best good news stories that I've heard in African conservation

We are talking a cliff which is, in many places, 1000 metres [3280 feet] high. So for an animal as sure-footed as a Walia, it's a confined environment, but in some ways it's about as protected as you can get. Humans just cannot utilize these cliffs. And I think the ideal situation would be to see Walia spread along to all of the cliff habitats that they could fill and live in, and then probably their numbers would stabilize. We're certainly a long way from getting to that level, but the Walia ibex is one of the few African animals that's on the right track.

CHADDEN HUNTER

The disappearing frogs

Few of us in Europe really understand the importance of frogs world-wide. I've just come back from Central America. In one small area in Panama, there are over 50 different species of frogs – and enormous numbers of them – because the moist, humid environment there particularly suits them. In many ways, they are the equivalent of small rodents in Europe – crucial links in the flow of energy along the food chain. And they are very vulnerable because they absorb substances through their moist skins and thus are easily infected by fungi. There's a fungus moving up Panama and the isthmus, which by next year will certainly have killed another two species. Now the concern is that the disappearance of these amphibians may cause complete disruption of the ecosystem. **DAVID ATTENBOROUGH**

Well, the interesting thing about Costa Rica is you can see imagery of huge stretches of apparently pristine mountain forest, and all is protected, and one thinks, well, that's fine – everything must be safe. But, of course, underneath, a lot of those frog populations have gone extinct or are crashing to extinction literally within months. There are major problems because of this new disease.

There's been a lot of forensic work to find where this fungus has come from, and it's now been traced back to the African clawed toad, which came out of South Africa. If you look at museum specimens, a certain proportion of them have the fungus in the skin, and it looks as if toads from South Africa were exported in the 1930s in very large numbers to hospitals in the Western world, because they're used as a biological indicator of human pregnancy, for hormone testing. Then presumably some have escaped, and that's how the fungus has got into the water systems. We're now still seeing the effects of its spread worldwide, even if we don't yet understand the exact means of water-borne transmission.

It's been seen to be coming. Monitoring in advance of a sort of moving wave of the arrival of the fungus shows it's moving at something like 30 kilometres [19 miles] a year through Central America.

It goes from year to year zero, zero, zero, and then suddenly there's a huge spike in the occurrence of the fungus, and the populations come crashing, literally, in months.

There's a huge amount of work going on in laboratories all over the place, trying to understand the impact of the chytrid fungus. But the problem, of course, is it's not the chytrid alone – it's the interaction of a whole series of factors.

ecosystems are being stressed, and we expect amphibians to be some of the earliest indicators of that stress

What's the relationship between the chytrid fungus spread and global climate change? We don't really know yet. Ecosystems are being stressed, and we expect amphibians to be some of the earliest indicators of that stress. But what are those stresses in those montane systems? Are they global issues of climate change or are they more local ones?

There's a very interesting case in the cloudforests of Monteverde in Costa Rica. A lot of their frogs have come crashing down to extinction. Why is that? Well, it may be that there's been deforestation at lower altitudes, so the heat relationships of the land there are quite different. Hot air is rising, and there's less cloud. The conditions are less optimal for those cloudforest frogs, and they are being stressed. Because they are being stressed, they're now perhaps more sensitive to the chytrid fungus. So we're dealing with an extraordinary interplay of factors affecting frogs, which we don't yet understand.

We're still in the epidemiological stage of it spreading, and we don't yet know where it's going to go. It's probably safest to assume it will spread worldwide, though there are examples of populations of some species that appear to be resistant.

The IUCN figure is that one third of all frogs at the moment are endangered. Of course, it's not as simple as that because, while some species are going extinct in front of our eyes, we're still discovering

> I think we are faced probably with the extinction of at least half the world's frogs ... this is the most urgent species-conservation issue of today

new ones. So it's a very dynamic situation, and the public finds that rather hard to understand – 'If you say there's a crisis with frogs, well why can't you tell us how many there are?' Because we're still discovering how the world works.

There's still a huge job of learning what biodiversity there is, and of course what the relationships are between frog species and their environment. So I think we are faced probably with the extinction of at least half the world's frogs. From the speed at which the fungus is spreading and the way it is popping up in new places, I think we shall see massive extinctions probably on a timescale of 10 years, 20 years. And so from the conservation point of view, this is the most urgent species-conservation issue of today.

MARK STANLEY PRICE

The shrinking polar bear

The polar bear is one of the most dramatic examples of a species that is directly suffering from climate change. Its habitat is undergoing a fundamental transformation. The pack ice upon which polar bears depend is retreating further and fuurther northwards in the Arctic. They depend on the pack ice because that's where the seals upon which they prey tend to live. As the pack ice retreats, the polar bears suffer. The ones that are seen are thinner. They're having fewer cubs. They're coming into more conflict with local people, entering villages that they avoided before. And the people who live in the same habitat with the polar bears, such as the Inuit, are suffering from a similar set of problems.

JEFF MCNEELY

It's perfectly clear that polar bears are less well nourished than they were. The incidence of triplets, for example, has gone down significantly. So we know that polar bears are under stress, and there seems very little doubt that if climate change proceeds and the ice retreats significantly more, polar bears will not be able to survive.   **DAVID ATTENBOROUGH**

There are 2.5 million ringed seals in the Arctic – an immense number. But they need to give birth to their pups under the snow or even on top of the ice. If there is no ice, then they would give birth to their pups in the water, and the pups would drown. So the loss of ice will affect them greatly. And if we lose ringed seals, that'll really impact the polar bears, because the number-one food source for polar bears is ringed seals.

So now that leaves the polar bear in a desperate situation. If there's no other food, they'll go to islands where walruses haul out and will attempt to hunt them. I have seen very young bears come to these islands where walrus herds haul out. I don't know if that's just very unusual, whether they're learning how to hunt walruses or if they're being forced to do this by desperation because they have nothing to eat. Maybe, the stress of climate change is forcing them to these islands to take a greater risk.

In the short term, walruses might have a bigger problem, because they eat clams. They mine a clam bed very quickly, and they can only go so far before they have to return to haul out again. If the season of open water lasts even longer, up to half the year, then the walruses might have nothing to eat.

What is different about the current situation with climate change is the amount of time that walrus herds will be stuck on these islands. They're a pinniped, they must haul out of the water, and when there's no ice, they have only one choice, to go to the islands. So with polar bears coming to these islands and them stuck together for a longer period of time, this is going to be very bad for walrus herds. In the short term it could be good for polar

> if we lose ringed seals, that'll really impact the polar bears, because the number-one food source for polar bears is ringed seals

bears. It'll give them that opportunity to eat, which they won't otherwise have. **ADAM RAVETCH**

The polar ice has always expanded and contracted. Can we do anything to keep a reservoir of polar bears, for example, in Spitzbergen, in
the Russian far north or in Canada? Maintaining even a modest reservoir
population of polar bears would provide the basis for adapting to the
return of polar sea ice at some point in the future.

I'm really worried about the polar bears. The estimates are that we
might lose 35 per cent of them over the next 50 years. And as their
population continues to decline and their prey species move further out
to sea, it's going to be a very tough adaptation for the polar bears.

JEFF MCNEELY

There are two possibilities – one, they go extinct as they try desperately
to find ice, or two, they may go further south and come onto firm land.
If they do that it's going to bring even more conflict with human communities, and of course their habits will have to change greatly. Maybe
they will evolve to do that. Maybe we will have a new species of terrestrial bear which looks like a polar bear but doesn't behave like the polar
bear that we have all grown up knowing.

Whether the polar bear can ever evolve to being a different sort of
bear on dry land, I don't think we know. What is interesting is that with
many animals you can probably predict
how they might behave, and bears are
generalists, omnivores in many places –
the brown bear is a relative omnivore
compared to the polar bear. So it might
indeed be possible for it to de-specialize.
Bears are probably pretty adaptable and
flexible, but it's got a very short time in
which to do this. If the projection is that
the polar ice cap will have disappeared
within 50 years, we are expecting an

> maybe we will have
> a new species of
> terrestrial bear which
> looks like a polar bear
> but doesn't behave
> like the polar bear
> that we have all
> grown up knowing

awful lot of a bear in the way of habitat change, annual movement change, feeding habits, hunting techniques. And, of course, the bear situation is a particularly interesting one, because if you think of its habitat as a large iceberg, that is something which we certainly cannot recreate.

MARK STANLEY PRICE

I think some bears will die in the southern Arctic region. I think the northern populations will move further north to try to find the ice, and in the short term, part of the polar bear population will survive. I'm always hopeful. I don't want to believe these predictions that polar bears might be extinct in 50 or 100 years. I've spent so much time in the field with them, I don't want to believe that. I'm much more optimistic and believe that they will adapt, and they will figure out where the food source is and find it, and survive.

ADAM RAVETCH

There's a very intimate connection between our worries about climate change and our worries about loss of biological diversity, because the impacts on biological diversity up to this point have derived essentially from three things: habitat destruction, over-exploitation – overharvesting – and introducion of alien species, and often two or sometimes all three. These are now being compounded by changes, not of our direct destruction of the habitat, but of global climate change, and you can measure with good documentation bird ranges changing, fish distributions changing, flowering seasons changing. And it's fairly clear that many organisms can't move fast enough naturally, or they can't move through intervening territory to where they want to be.

What that means for many of the nature reserves and wilderness areas that we've set aside is that insofar as they were chosen particularly to focus on some set of endangered species, they're no longer going to be fit for purpose. So there are interplays like that.

If your large chunks of the Amazonian rainforest depend on a great deal of precipitation, and if climate changes those precipitation patterns, then you're in serious trouble, and that has feedbacks itself on the climate change. Some of these are things we understand clearly, and some of them are things we don't understand quite so well.

On the other hand, if one takes the really long view, one has to realize that marine mammals have, if you look at them on the sweep of millions of years, had good times and bad times, and there are times when it's been much colder and times when it's been warmer. So although we will lose species, unfolding on the sweep of millions of years will be changes, and maybe new interesting things will happen.

I see this as no comfort, because what is really different about this event and all previous events is that climate change is being folded together with the already huge impact of humans, which was already causing massive extinctions. So, yes, maybe 10 million years from now there'll be an interesting and different world, but that's not usually what people are thinking about when they talk about conservation biology.

ROBERT MAY

what is really different about this event and all previous events is that climate change is being folded together with the already huge impact of humans, which was already causing massive extinctions

Climate change is probably a bigger threat than almost everything else we're doing to life on Earth combined. If you really look at what happens under natural climate change and then try to imagine how it would happen today in these highly modified landscapes, which are basically obstacle courses, we're setting up a huge wave of extinctions.

THOMAS LOVEJOY

It's interesting if you look at climate research. There are people looking at models, trying to simulate, trying to predict all the time. I don't see enough research on the biological world happening. What is it going to look like?

We know that boundaries will be shifted. We know that the population status of the Galapagos penguin depends on sea temperature, because of the food supply. But if the El Niño events are happening too often, the penguin can't repopulate – its numbers can't go up. Well, therefore it needs to move into waters that are cooler. But where will that be? It lives at the moment on a very isolated oceanic archipelago. There is no further land suitable, say, 1000 miles [1610 kilometres] further north. So what are we going to do? Do we look for an equivalent place in the southern hemisphere – the same latitude, same currents – and release them there? Do we try to preserve what we see as natural, in our very narrow time perspective, or do we say we are actually interested in having functioning, self-sustaining populations in the 'wild'?

I don't think anyone's doing the thinking on this yet. We are all desperately scrambling with the proximate issues, while we should be putting more effort into planning and visioning, imagineering for those future scenarios.

MARK STANLEY PRICE

we are all desperately scrambling with the proximate issues, while we should be putting more effort into planning and visioning

On Loving Wilderness

4

There can't be a human culture that does not derive some inspiration from wilderness, whether it's through the perceived purity of nature or the spiritual experience of being away from human society and alone with the rest of the world. So does this mean we have an innate love of wilderness and nature – or 'biophilia', as Professor E.O. Wilson has called it? And what actually qualifies as wilderness, what is the overall effect of it on the individual human and on humanity as a whole, and where is its place in the hierarchy of human values?

The term wilderness has its origins in Norse languages and it apparently comes from 'will', which is 'uncontrolled', and 'deor', which means 'animal'. So it's an area where animals are uncontrolled and therefore an area where human intervention is at a minimum or doesn't exist at all.   **RUSSELL MITTERMEIER**

The word 'wilderness' is used in many ways. Some people use it to mean areas that have no human inhabitants. But I think actually it's more relevant in reference to undisturbed nature – tracts of forest or grassland or ocean which are largely untouched by human activity.

If you think about it in those terms, it means essential nature, nature as it was before we got too much in the way. If we're trying to conserve the basic systems which support life, it's important that some parts are wholly intact, that they have all the species that were originally there and that they can maintain the health of the whole system – it is biologically necessary. In any habitat, a cornerstone of long-term conservation is to have some pieces of that habitat that are essentially pristine.

JAMES LEAPE

To me, wilderness means something that is unfamiliar to us. I remember the first time I went to Borneo. We were searching for orang-utans, walking through the forest and looking with binoculars into the tops of the trees. This was virgin wilderness. And after an hour or so, looking up and not watching where I was going, I tripped over the remains of a brick wall. It was the remnant of an ancient settlement, in this virgin wilderness, from the time of the Srivijaya kingdom, over 1500 years ago. So wilderness certainly doesn't mean that no people ever lived there.

People have lived everywhere, except of course Antarctica, and have influenced wilderness wherever we see it. So I think of wilderness as a state of mind. Maybe it's a place where we feel out of place, where our civilization offers little support and where we no longer feel in control of our own destiny.

I think of wilderness as a state of mind. Maybe it's a place where we feel out of place, where our civilization offers little support and where we no longer feel in control of our own destiny

Based on that definition, there's quite a lot of wilderness around. I think for some people, like the San bushmen of the Kalahari, New York City would be a wilderness.

JEFF MCNEELY

How would I define wilderness? Well I can do it geographically in the same way that the organization that I'm affiliated with, Conservation International, has done it: so many thousand square kilometres, so much undisturbed vegetation cover on it. A piece of land has to be fairly substantial to be a typical wilderness. But generally speaking, what I see as wilderness is an extensive amount of land, probably at least hundreds of thousands of square kilometres, that is complex, contains the original fauna and flora – at least a large part of it – and is left strictly alone, except for visits.   E.O. WILSON

people are starting to realize that natural areas where people are not the dominant force necessarily are of great value

Wilderness is a concept that has been developed mainly in western society, and it recognizes that there are certain places that have either very low human populations or are entirely devoid of people. It's very much used in the US and the UK, in a few other European countries and, of course, in Australia, which was one of the pioneers of the concept, but it is a concept that hasn't necessarily been adopted world-wide. Yet it's something that I think is increasingly becoming important on an ever more overcrowded planet. I think that people are starting to realize that natural areas where people are not the dominant force necessarily are of great value.   RUSSELL MITTERMEIER

Wilderness is a term which is used differently by different people. So for some people, wilderness might literally be their back garden, and for others, who are thinking maybe on a global scale, wilderness might be one of the big deserts – such as the Gobi Desert or the Sahara Desert. It might be the Arctic, it might be the mountain systems of the world – the Himalayas or the Andes, for example.

maybe the only true wildernesses are those at the bottom of the deep seas

But in reality, almost every surface of the planet can be seen and has been mapped by satellite, and so maybe the only true wildernesses are those at the bottom of the deep seas. There we don't know what's going on.

We don't know what's living there. We don't know how the system works there.

NEVILLE ASH

Wilderness is a very problematic term. I remember when an American writer did a survey of people's attitude towards wilderness, one child replied, 'Wilderness is the dark space under my bed.' Even before humans had started to dramatically change the climate, and therefore the whole biology of the planet, DDT was being found in the livers of Antarctic penguins. So there's no sense in which any corner of the planet can now be called a wilderness in the simple definition of the term – that is, somewhere completely uncontaminated or untouched by human beings.

RICHARD MABEY

How does being in wilderness affect you?

When filming for *Planet Earth*, I went to the Gobi Desert in Mongolia, an area the size of Holland, and we, the crew, were the only people we ever saw there.

The feeling of being in a true wilderness is a difficult emotion to get across. Ultimately you feel free – not influenced by humans – and you know that everything you're seeing is natural. You know what you're seeing is probably how it's always been.

When you live in the modern world like we do, there's nothing around you that is really natural. Of course there's wildlife around. There are birds singing now, but I can also hear the distant sounds of a car. You can stand in a wilderness like the Gobi Desert and hear no other human sounds. That makes you feel very different about the world.

HUW CORDEY

The place that I'm really passionate about is Antarctica. One of the wonderful things about it is the silence. It's often very, very quiet. You never hear a combustion engine, which is almost impossible on most of our planet. You also feel terribly small – the scale of everything, and the ability of the weather to change so dramatically in one day. It can be a beautiful, sunlit day and then suddenly – often within a matter of hours – you're actually in real danger. It's a place where you just feel terribly small, and that is a wonderful thing. It put me and, in a sense, it puts humans very much back in place.   **ALASTAIR FOTHERGILL**

What does wilderness mean to us spiritually and emotionally?

there is something about the wonder of nature, nature in its infinite variety and mystery that touches people in their souls

There is something about the wonder of nature, nature in its infinite variety and mystery that touches people in their souls. For all the talk about the ecological value of species, about the value of ecosystems to our own survival – which is very real – it's important to remember that nature is wonderful and that, for many people, it is something to be treasured.   **JAMES LEAPE**

Every major religion, I think, has roots in the wilderness and imperatives and impulses within it that lead it back towards the wilderness. It's as if, in that context – where human needs and human plans are so relativized, where you feel so appropriately small – the overwhelmingness of the divine comes home in quite fresh ways.

One of the things wilderness says to us is that nature is not just there for us to be comfortable in. There's an element of the world around us, a profound element and an extensive element, that is just there. It's there for its own sake. It is what it is. And wilderness always tells us the world isn't just designed for us to build houses in, or have holidays and gardens. And in that sense, I think wilderness always speaks to humans of transcendence, in the widest possible sense. It says, 'You as a human being are part of the system which is not just about your needs and your concerns. Like it or not, you're part of something immense and very mysterious.'

like it or not, you're part of something immense and very mysterious

The recognition that there's always around the corner something which is not yours and nothing to do with you is part of locating us in the real world. People talk about living in the real world sometimes, and frequently the people who do that when they're talking about economics, for instance, seem to me most emphatically not living in the real world, because the real world is a world of excess and mysteriousness and strangeness and challenge, which the wilderness represents very eloquently to us.

ROWAN WILLIAMS, ARCHBISHOP OF CANTERBURY

All the great monastic traditions – whether Christian, Buddhist or Daoist – all find their roots in an experience of their founders going into the desert, into the wilderness, onto the mountains, and finding there something that civilization cannot give them – a realization about them-selves, about nature, about the divine. You go into the wilderness to find God and to find yourself. In the monastic tradition of Irish and Welsh Christianity, for example, from the fourth to the tenth century AD, you went into the most desolate places to get away from the trappings of so-called civilization but also to find God and to find yourself.

The Taoists in China have exactly the same thing, and they have a won-derful symbol for the immortal – in fact, a Chinese character – for the person who has achieved absolute spiritual perfection: a human being alone on a mountain. The Taoist definition of

the Taoists ... have a wonderful ... Chinese character – for the person who has achieved absolute spiritual perfection: a human being alone on a mountain

enlightenment is to be away from everything. So for the faiths, wilderness is a place of engagement where, within the religious world, you expose yourself to nature without defences, without any attempt to interpret or to control. It's a place where you go to discover more about yourself, possibly more about nature and maybe even something more about the cosmos and beyond. It's the ultimate existentialist adventure, and that is why so many sacred sites are set there. **MARTIN PALMER**

one of the great illusions of our culture is that somehow we live in a bubble which really insulates us from all that

We launched a church consultation document a couple of years ago on the environment, in which in the introduction it was said: 'One of the things we can most usefully do, simply to raise our environmental awareness, is go and get in touch – quite literally – go and get wet in a shower of rain. Go and dig the garden. Go and be tactile.' We still have these things which reacquaint us with that real world of unmanageable material out there, and one of the great illusions of our culture is that somehow we live in a bubble which really insulates us from all that. And that's why I think rain is very good for all of us. It just tells us there's nothing you can do about it. If you're in a shower of rain, you get wet, and that's something of great spiritual profundity.

ROWAN WILLIAMS, ARCHBISHOP OF CANTERBURY

There is not a single religion in the world – and UNEP has convened a number of meetings between religion and environment – which has not put the protection of the environment at the heart of the values of that religion: be it Christianity, be it the Jewish faith, Buddhism or Islam. For example, in Africa, you have forests that are considered as sacred, so they are protected. This comes back to the indigenous people and their relationship with nature. They have respected each and every living organism – if it is there, God has created it, and therefore it has a value.

AHMED DJOGHLAF

We're all part of God's creation, that's the wonder of it. The problem is in the West we've become so tarmacked over, if I could put it that way, that we've lost that sense of the beauty of creation, the wonder of nature. There's nothing better I think than to go out into the country-side and simply sit down quietly and absorb the beauty and the wonder of creation – to just sit and absorb the wonder that all this has been created by God for our benefit and for our use. But he's also said to us you are stewards of the creation and the nature I've given you.

I know some people don't like that term steward, but I think it's a very good one, because what does a steward do? What is his job? He is given the goods, but he must look after them with prudence. He has to distribute them fairly. He has to have a concern for the common good of all those he's serving. And so, in that sense, theologically and from a Catholic point of view, we are the stewards of creation, and we need to understand the rhythms of nature, so that we don't exhaust through selfishness and overconsumption the natural resources which God has given us.   **PETER SMITH, ROMAN CATHOLIC ARCHBISHOP OF CARDIFF**

We've just done a project where we've looked at the importance of sacred sites in wilderness preservation, because many of the most important wilderness areas are also sacred mountains, sacred deserts, sacred valleys, sacred rivers, and there is a very direct relationship in the religious world between the sacred and the wilderness.

We asked Oxford and Harvard universities, with their palaeobotany sections, 'Can you find out for us whether these sites were biodiverse before they became sacred or whether they became more biodiverse because they are sacred?' And the evidence seems to show that, in many parts of the world, by making something sacred – a mountain, a river, a plain – it actually protects it, gives it a sense of sanctuary, and

by making something sacred – a mountain, a river, a plain – it actually protects it, gives it a sense of sanctuary, and creatures can live there undisturbed we've had Buddhist monks assassinated because they went into areas where loggers wanted to go, and by making them sacred, the loggers could no longer go in

creatures can live there undisturbed because you don't tend to go and hunt or log on a sacred site.

But that's a passive protection. It's because it's sacred it isn't harmed. What we've done with many of the world's religions is to say, 'Let's identify, with the environmentalists, the most endangered areas and let's go and make them sacred. Let's stick a temple in there, or a church or a cross or a shrine or a statue,' and the effect is astonishing. Local people actually view the government as somebody who you try and outwit, and therefore you don't care what the regulations are; you also don't care what the United Nations has said about protecting biodiversity. But if you think you're going to be cursed, you're going to get ill or you're going to have misfortune, or you just don't want to basically upset the deities, that's a far stronger reason for protecting.

So what we've done is to take something that works and say let's make it work even more strongly by putting it where it needs to be to protect wilderness and forests. This has been costly: we've had Buddhist monks assassinated because they went into areas where loggers wanted to go, and by making them sacred, the loggers could no longer go in. It's powerful stuff. This is not just superstition, this is actually why some places still are beautiful and sacred. Now, we're setting out to make many more sacred places and, God willing, they'll also remain beautiful. **MARTIN PALMER**

Wilderness psychology is an extension of that notion of an existence which is beyond ours. If you were to go beyond simplistic considerations of the usefulness of wildlife, that we might possibly find a cure for cancer in other forms of life – if you get beyond that and actually start being a bit more grown-up, can we say that the life systems of a planet have got a value in their own right? I think ethically that they do, and

I think, as a species, we have to move towards recognising that we must value other organisms and the systems that they live in simply because they're there.

RICHARD MABEY

I think wilderness has a great spiritual value to us, and we're fascinated with it. We've been fascinated since the earliest days of exploration. I think many of us also feel that it has a great aesthetic value, too. Many of us feel a moral obligation to conserve it, and I think that we also need to look at it in terms of the great range of ecosystem services that it provides to global society. And, as someone who's worked a lot with indigenous people, I think that maintaining large areas of wilderness is critical to the survival of many of these unique and very special indigenous groups that still co-exist with us on this planet, including a number of uncontacted tribes.

RUSSELL MITTERMEIER

We have to remember that humans have evolved as hunter-gatherers. In fact, 99 per cent of our existence on Earth was spent as a hunter-gatherer entirely reliant on wild resources. One of the great generalizations we can make about hunter-gatherers, whether they're in the Siberian tundra or the Amazonian rainforest, is that they very much see themselves as an integral part of a finely tuned ecosystem. They are merely one part of it. They see themselves as borrowing resources from it and ultimately redistributing it, and their stories and myths reinforce this element – when it's appropriate to kill an animal, who's appropriate to kill it, how it's distributed, and therefore the ecological effects. So it's never a

to a hunter-gatherer, the world is part of a complex cosmological whole, a universe, if you like, of which they are a small, integral part

simple matter of kill the animal and eat some of it.

I think it's fair to say that no hunter-gatherer would ever view an animal or a sheaf of wheat as simply being a resource. Normally living things are imbued with a lot more meaning, and certainly issues of wastage or over-exploitation would probably be wrapped up in these sorts of meanings. But the important point is that these are holistic environments in which there are complex and changing relationships between resource and user.

To a hunter-gatherer, the world is part of a complex cosmological whole, a universe, if you like, of which they are a small, integral part. Wherever one looks among hunter-gatherers past or present, the cosmological whole is the critical thing. No-one exists in a vacuum as a hunter-gatherer, or indeed a small-scale agriculturalist, and this is obviously what humans have lost as we've come through this technological arms race, as we've increased our population significantly, as we've complexified throughout the course of the past 5000–6000 years. We've distanced ourselves from any spiritual relationship with the world.

Our religions have become anthropocentric. They are geared towards what we do and what we do in the hereafter, and they have therefore relegated the resources of the Earth to being mere adjuncts to support humans, which are the be all and end all of life on Earth, and so on.

Clearly this disjuncture, this spiritual disjuncture underpins – I wouldn't say is responsible for – but underpins much of our very rash thinking about the way we interact with the world.   **PAUL PETTITT**

There is a link between extinction of species and the weakening of our heritage. There is a close link between the richness of a culture and the richness of its biodiversity. And when we lose the biodiversity, we lose at the same time the cultural value of the citizens and the civilization and our relationship with the nature. According to UNESCO, we have more or less 6000 languages in the world. Half of them will disappear because our natural environment is shrinking, including the words. Words disappear because you don't use them – because a plant, an animal is disappearing. Therefore we need to address this issue of environment not only in terms of money – money is important – but also in terms of it as part of our heritage and part of ourselves.

You cannot approach the future and address the present without knowing your past.

AHMED DJOGHLAF

There are still many indigenous people around the world, and the only places where they have any chance of maintaining some semblance of their traditional lifestyles are in these wilderness areas. Many of them have existed traditionally in very small human populations occupying extensive areas and can't live in an area that's been largely urbanized or impacted. A lot of their future is linked to the future of wilderness areas.

RUSSELL MITTERMEIER

Until about 5000 years ago, most humans would have lived in small groups, they probably would have had a blood relationship to most humans they came into contact with. They certainly probably recognized most people, and they would have an intimate association with the killing of animals, the reaping of crops. In other words, they would be plugged in to the everyday experience of staying alive.

a lot of our culture is grown from the emotional response we have to nature

This would be so whether or not they actually played a role in killing those cows or harvesting the corn and so on. It's only when humans begin to aggregate in relatively large, complex urban societies, let's say in Egypt, Mesopotamia, India, that for the first time they begin to be disassociated from this everyday experience – the meat you start seeing is in the butcher's window rather than on the field.

This must inevitably have a significant role in how humans perceive the landscape. It must begin that process of distancing us. So it is a phenomenon of urban societies, of complex societies in which people are specialized enough that they don't need to do a bit of everything to survive.   **PAUL PETTITT**

There's a lot of evidence that human beings need life, are attracted to life forms, and a lot of our culture is grown from the emotional response we have to nature. So there is the spiritual argument for looking after the creation. Biodiversity is a creation that should be of as much concern to everyone, including religious people, as it is to the scientists who study it.   **E.O. WILSON**

somewhere inside most humans, certainly when they are children, a sense persists of what Edward Wilson called 'biophilia', an affiliation with the natural world

I think wild places and the things that live in them have always moved human beings, moved them out of affection and wonder and fear. Maybe one of the greatest losses we have come to as a species is a kind of softening of those emotions, so that it's now amusement and pleasure and entertainment we get from wild things, rather than those fundamental emotions that early peoples had. I've always been fascinated by very early cave paintings, which are the first kind of emotional and spiritual responses which human beings made in solid form. The cave paintings were the first images that humans created, and the things which they chose to represent were not invented gods or their fellow human beings, they were other creatures. They were plainly fascinated by them, fascinated by their vivacity, their ability to reappear as the seasons moved.

Through all the terrible abuses that human beings have committed against the natural world in the thousands of years since those cave paintings were made, I still look back to that moment with fantastic optimism and believe a choice was made, that those creatures out there in some way belonged to the same world as the humans looking at them and were worth celebrating. That bond which was first expressed in those cave paintings has continued. Somewhere inside most humans, certainly when they are children, a sense persists of what Edward Wilson called 'biophilia', an affiliation with the natural world.

> somewhere inside most humans, certainly when they are children, a sense persists of what Edward Wilson called 'biophilia', an affiliation with the natural world

I would tend always to be an optimist in these things and say that that is the natural state. It's what we came out of – and it is the severance, the alienation, the abuse of nature that is the oddity, the anomaly that's a result of certain things in civilization and urban living and agriculture.

RICHARD MABEY

Do humans have an innate biophilia? I think so, yes. Watch children and you will see – right from the very, very earliest age – an interest and an excitement about the natural world. They are as interested in a worm retracting into a hole as they are in a displaying chaffinch, or indeed watching tadpoles change from curious little wriggling fish-like things to things with four legs.

> it's in our nature to be concerned about the nature of life around us, and to be fascinated by it

It's in our nature to be concerned about the nature of life around us, and to be fascinated by it. Of course as we get older, sadly, some people lose touch with the natural world around them altogether. But if they do, it's a major loss.

DAVID ATTENBOROUGH

Why does man seek wilderness? This is pure speculation, but we know enough now from what has come to be called evolutionary psychology or environmental psychology to be reasonably sure that there are some

when people say, 'Humans are happy living in a city, in the rat race ... I say, 'Well, yes, up to a point. But so is a cow or a pig in a stall, being raised for meat, kept fed, warm and happy.'

very deep desires in the human psyche that amount to almost instincts, and they include the need to expand, to explore, to approach the unknown. This is an impulse that comes particularly when people have taken care of their most basic needs. They have sustenance, and now they want entertainment, and they want more than that – they want adventure, they want a sense of the unknown. They'd like to be part, even if vicariously, of exploring untrammelled areas. When they can't get it in any way that seems practicable, then they dream about it, such as finding other planets with alien life. It's just natural to human beings, and I don't think that that's strictly a contrivance of Western civilization.

Would other animals wish the same? I don't know what goes on in the minds of other animals, but I suspect that there are emotions that make animals more lively when they get into an open, new environment with lots of new resources that are basically the same that have moved our ancestors for thousands of generations. However, we have through culture elevated it to a new level of complexity and sensitivity – it is a great tree of emotions and impulses and aesthetic stimulation. The wilderness and the nature that goes with it has come from deep roots in human ancestry, and we're tampering with it, and we're trimming it off and disposing of it at our peril.

When people say, 'Humans are happy living in a city, in the rat race of a suburb,' and so on, I say, 'Well, yes, up to a point. But so is a cow or a pig in a stall, being raised for meat, kept fed, warm and happy.' That's a long way from a real, original cow, a cattle species, or a wild pig. They lived in a totally different environment and they have instincts and feelings probably, too, that can never be developed, much less felt because they've been put in that constricted environment. E.O. WILSON

There's a great deal of talk these days about the value of contact with the natural world for human health, which is fine, but I think it's in danger of becoming sentimental and simplistic and a bit like the old kind of eighteenth-century pastoral image of the rustic world as pretty and comforting. Sometimes the natural world can provide images of prettiness and beauty, but it can also be very funny. It can be profoundly tragic. It can be full of poignancy and unsolved problems.

I think if you open yourself up to the kind of currents of life and imagination that are flowing through the natural world, you can find them flowing through yourself as well. This is not to be anthropomorphic. It is not to say at all that human beings are trying to see other animals as images of themselves. Almost exactly the reverse: to truly engage with wildness is possibly to discover the wild animal in oneself, and I think this, too, can be a source of great learning.

RICHARD MABEY

Why should we care about wilderness?

Well, the simplest answer is that this is one planet at the end of the day. That's perhaps a very utilitarian answer, but it's not a bad place to start. It's not as if any bit of the world is hermetically sealed off from any other. What happens at the North Pole will have a practical impact on what happens in central London. It's not as if there's some miraculous protection around urban, Western, prosperous society that'll save it from the basic effects of environmental disaster.

I think, at a deeper level, just accepting that the universe is more than the one we can see and use and manage is spiritually and morally very significant for people, whether they live in Kensington or in Greenland. **ROWAN WILLIAMS, ARCHBISHOP OF CANTERBURY**

Why should we care about the wild places and the welfare of the world? The word stewardship is used a great deal, and it has a real meaning, for we are now the most powerful species the world has ever seen, and we now have it in our hands to destroy pretty well anything. We should therefore take on the moral responsibility of being the stewards of the planet on which we happen to have developed.   **DAVID** ATTENBOROUGH

Why does wilderness matter? At this moment in history, you'd have to answer that in two ways: why does it matter for all the things that live in it, and why does it matter for us? The ideal answer, which we need to work towards, is to answer those two questions simultaneously.

Big wild places are profoundly important, not just because they are very often the locations of interesting forms of life, but also because in these great wildernesses, which haven't yet been processed and simplified by human management, there is still the opportunity for wild systems to work out solutions to things like climate change. And if they are big enough, I'm rather optimistic about their ability to use the accumulated intelligence of thousands of millions of years of evolution to start ducking and diving a bit. They're actually rather cleverer at looking after the planet than we are. But you need space to do that. You need the opportunity for creatures to migrate and change their living relationships one with another. And they can't do that in small places or in places where the rules of the game have been set by humans and not by the wild system. So I think that in terms of the future survival of the planet, the existence of these big wild places where the rules of the game are ancient, not set by humans, may be very important for the survival of us all.

In terms of the value of wildernesses for humans, they're arenas where we can meditate upon what it means to be human, because you can't understand what it means to be human until you truly understand

> these big wild places where the rules of the game are ancient, not set by humans, may be very important for the survival of us all

what it means to be non-human or greater-than-human, as American deep-ecologists call it.

When you begin to appreciate the possibility that there are other ways of living on the Earth than the way that we live, then I think it makes one a better human. It makes one aware of one's own strengths as a species and one's weaknesses, and how perhaps one should give way at times to the demands of other organisms – not only for their sake but because perhaps it'd make us better as well. So I think there are those two levels: the psychological experience of wilderness and the ecological experience of it, which would be lovely to bring together into a holistic sense.

RICHARD MABEY

you can't understand what it means to be human until you truly understand what it means to be non-human or greater-than-human

It comes down really to choice. We need wildernesses in order to give human beings choice. If we humanize the planet completely, if we cover it with our cities and our suburbs, if we trammel every square foot of the Earth and mark it off and put fences around it and map it completely and alter it totally from the way it was when humanity first appeared several million years ago, then we have closed out the choices for future generations, all of them to come. If we can keep open wilderness areas – that is, wide stretches of land where, as the American Wilderness Act of 1964 put it, humanity does not live but can visit, and when done, leaves – then we will have saved the part of the Earth that helped form, through human evolution, the way the human mind works. That offers a choice that really should be part of the birthright of every human being ultimately – to be given freely and realized, if not in the current generation because

if we trammel every square foot of the Earth ... then we have closed out the choices for future generations, all of them to come

of the poor economic condition of most of the world's population, then for future generations to come.　　　　　**E.O. WILSON**

What happens if we don't re-engage with the wild? I think it might be a very dismal prospect. The assumption that we can, as it were, sit round like members of a planetary committee and work out what's going to happen to the world in the state of crisis, purely from scientific reason, is preposterous.

> the assumption that we can, as it were, sit round like members of a planetary committee and work out what's going to happen to the world in the state of crisis, purely from scientific reason, is preposterous

Before we have any hope of devising practical solutions, we need to make a massive emotional leap of empathy. We need to get down off that assumption that we are in charge of the planet and can do that kind of managerial job, and to recognize that we are really rather ill-educated members of a planetary democracy, no better and no more important than algae or baboons or *Stipa* grass.

Unless we make that leap – which is both a moral leap and, I think, an emotional one – I don't think we're going to make much progress.　　　**RICHARD MABEY**

You look out, and the sea is beautiful. It moves you. But if you could look through it and see what was going on underneath – if you could see the bottom where some trawler had recently been trawling – it would be like someone had been gardening with a bulldozer. Yes, you could raise vegetables with a bulldozer, but it would be a pretty clumsy way of going about it. The destruction which is being wrought by humanity on the oceans is so total, so vast – and so completely beyond the comprehension of most people, because all of it is covered up by this lovely, emotive surface.

Of course, even if you could see down through the surface, a lot of the damage would still be invisible. Most pollutants can't be seen at all. But they're there, they're working 24 hours a day, and they're causing problems that must be attended to. We have to stop letting such pollutants get into the sea.

Up until now science has ruled the roost in terms of what takes place in conservation around the world. We need to expand from there. We need to bring in the humanities – poetry, art, music, dance – everything and anything that will make a difference in how people view this problem, because this problem matters. It matters to their lives, it matters to their hearts, it matters in every way.

Humpback whales are the whales that sing the loveliest songs. They change their songs and they use rhyme in the songs that are most complicated. They do all sorts of wonderful things with their young – they play games and they are tolerant in a way which just blows your mind if you've been a parent of four children, as I have. For two years I spent all my time talking to writers, artists, musicians – anybody who would listen – to try to bring whales into the human culture, because I felt that's what we need most. We need a presence of these magnificent creatures in our lives.

ROGER PAYNE

After all that's said and done, this planet is still the only place where we know with certainty that life exists. Many of these wilderness areas are so rich in life, they're so special, that I think many people feel good about something like that being out there, even if they never get a chance to see it themselves.

I like to compare it to the whole issue of uncontacted peoples. If you look at the Amazon, there are at least 40 to 50 groups of uncontacted people still living in remote corners. I'm pretty sure I'll never see one of those groups, and I don't want to because I don't want to interrupt their lives, which are complicated enough as it is. And yet the fact that on this planet in the twenty-first century we still have uncontacted peoples living traditional lifestyles, that's very special. **RUSSELL MITTERMEIER**

it turns out that most of the major problems we face are actually solvable, that the solutions are simple and that these solutions can take place using basic scientific information that we already have

Our lives contain a terrible paradox. We love nature, we are totally dependent on nature, yet we destroy nature.

What we need now to realize is that we can remedy a lot of the trouble we're causing. It turns out that most of the major problems we face are actually solvable, that the solutions are simple and that these solutions can take place using basic scientific information that we already have. We can start the process. We need to do that. It's really important.

We have to move. Margaret Mead, the famous anthropologist, was once asked if it was really possible for a single person or small group of people to change the world? To which she responded: 'It is the only thing that ever has changed the world.'

ROGER PAYNE

Wilderness and Usefulness

Wilderness is beautiful, inspirational and endowed with many other qualities that don't instantly bring hard-nosed economics to mind, but with a growing human population needing more and more natural resources, why should we preserve wild places rather than exploit them? Why should we care about uninhabitable tundra or deserts? We are just beginning to understand the real, and immense, value of goods and services that natural ecosystems provide, and economists can now put a price on these benefits. But will that make wilderness more cherished than ever or just turn it into another commodity to be traded?

What *is* wilderness?

Well, there are many different definitions for wilderness, and when we did our book on wilderness a few years ago, we chose a definition that's really a relative one. We recognized that, at a global level, wilderness areas need to be large. So we said they had to be at minimum 10,000 square kilometres or about a million hectares [2.47 million acres], and that they had to have a low human population density, less than five people per square kilometre, and that they had to have at least 70 per cent of the natural vegetation remaining intact.

Using that definition, 44 per cent of the Earth's land surface is still wilderness. What's more interesting, if we looked at those areas that had one person or less per square kilometre, we came up with 39 per cent of Earth's land surface. That's only about 43 million people, about 0.7 per cent of the world's human population in an area of nearly 40 per cent of the land surface of the planet. So there are a lot of places out there that have very few people.

That area surprised us. You have to recognize that about a third of it is permanent ice – Antarctica is huge, about 14 million square kilometres [5.4 million square miles] – about one and a half times the size of the US and almost as large as Russia, and of course the human population there is trivial. But the other two thirds, places like Amazonia and a number of other wilderness areas, also have very low populations, and they're rich in biodiversity.   **RUSSELL MITTERMEIER**

Areas that can still be called wilderness, quite frankly, are there because humanity hasn't been able to get into them and destroy them yet, for the most part. We do have parks and reserves and an increasing number of those, but generally, up to the era when conservation practice became part of national and global policy maybe 100 years ago, what was left of wilderness was simply that which we hadn't got to yet and destroyed. Even today when I take field trips looking for forest, particularly tropical forest – even here in the US – I have to aim for deep ravines and remote places. Those are the places that haven't been logged yet because it wasn't profitable to do so.   **E.O. WILSON**

> areas that can still be called wilderness, quite frankly, are there because humanity hasn't been able to get into them and destroy them yet

How fast is wilderness disappearing?

We do need to worry, because many of these areas are being heavily impacted by human activities. If you look 10, 20, 50 years down the line, many of these areas are going to lose their wilderness status. Even if the human population is very low in some of these wilderness areas, if you go in and you engage in a wide variety of forms of exploitation like completely unsustainable logging activities or mining activities, you can have a very heavy impact. **RUSSELL MITTERMEIER**

We're losing habitat very quickly at the moment, and we have done for quite a long time. So, for example, we've lost about half of the world's forest systems over the last 300 years, but the pattern of loss through that time has been very different. Much of the earlier period of loss was of temperate forests, especially in Europe and North America.

we're losing tropical forests at rates never seen before in the history of humankind

More recently, we're losing tropical forests at rates never seen before in the history of humankind. And in recent years, in the last decade or so, the amount of temperate forest has actually increased in Europe, North America and parts of northern Asia. **NEVILLE ASH**

In the 1980s in particular, there was a big surge in interest in tropical deforestation with a lot of media coverage and governmental attention being paid to, for example, the destruction of the Amazon-basin rain-forests. A lot of money has been spent and a lot of time and effort has gone into trying to identify ways to protect what's left, but sadly the deforestation continues, and in some countries at quite alarming rates. For example, in Indonesia, across the islands of Sumatra and Borneo, palm-oil plantations and logging are leading to vast swathes of forest still being cut down. **TONY JUNIPER**

The green wildernesses of the world are disappearing at a worrying pace. But protected areas are increasing at a remarkable pace, and so there's really a give and take on this. As some areas are losing wilderness, other areas are gaining. The eastern part of the US, for example, was almost totally deforested 200 years ago, and now it's been reforested and repopulated by black bears and moose. China is actually gaining forest area, no longer losing it. But China is harvesting everybody else's forest, and so wilderness is being lost in other parts of the world as a consequence of China's forest conservation policy.

We're all seriously concerned about the island of New Guinea as a place that has tremendous endemism – species found nowhere else – but very weak systems of management, and that's the kind of situation where vast areas of forest can be quickly lost to predatory logging companies. Places where the governments have control, where they manage areas well, are much less of a worry. Brazil is a huge country with rich resources and variable governance – a place where crops like soybeans are going to be expanding further and further into the Amazon, as the demand for soybeans for local biofuel or food exports to China continues to expand. So even though wilderness is doing better in some places, we ought to be seriously worried about the loss of wilderness at the global scale. **JEFF MCNEELY**

The disappearance of wilderness varies tremendously from place to place. Even within the Amazon region, certain portions are still in very good condition and are likely to be maintained over at least the next few decades, whereas others are rapidly being converted for other uses like cattle pasture and soy. So you're seeing, in certain places in the southern and southeastern Amazon and parts of the central Amazon, very rapid conversion. On the other hand, in the northern extremes of the Amazon, the border between Surinam and French Guiana, Guyana, southern Venezuela and the northern extremes of Brazil, are magnificent wilderness areas with very, very few people living in them. We're working very much now to ensure that those areas are maintained intact.

if any tropical rainforest areas remain intact 100 years from now, it's going to be in that very northern portion of Amazonia

There's an effort under way in all of those countries to set aside very large protected areas – trans-boundary protected areas or at least areas that are contiguous to one another across international borders. I believe that if any tropical rainforest areas remain intact 100 years from now, it's going to be in that very northern portion of Amazonia – what I like to refer to as the Brazil-Guianas Borderlands. So, even within one wilderness area, there's a great deal of variability in terms of the degree of loss.

RUSSELL MITTERMEIER

It's important to think about how much we have dammed the world's wild rivers. Just 50 years ago, around 1950, we had 5000 large dams around the world. Today we have 45,000, which means we've been building, on average, two large dams every day for half a century. This is a very, very large change in the hydrologic environment in a very short period of time. So, all of the aquatic life, all the species, all the creatures that are living in rivers are now dealing with a flow regime, a pattern of flow, that's very different from the one they've become adapted to.

There are big reservoirs on these rivers, and the releases from those reservoirs have a lot more to do with when farmers need to irrigate, when hydroelectric power needs to be produced, when water supplies need to be delivered, than with when fish need to migrate or spawn. So there have been serious habitat losses as a consequence of dams and reservoirs on these major rivers.

SANDRA POSTEL

How much wilderness do we need?

Right now we have about 13 per cent of the land cover designated as protected areas, specifically to conserve biodiversity and natural ecosystems. You might ask, is 13 per cent enough? And the answer to that is, it all depends. It depends essentially on how the areas around that 13 per cent are being managed. If we manage the rest of the land-scape in a thoughtful way, then 13 per cent may well be enough. If we overuse and abuse the rest of the landscape, then 13 per cent is nowhere near enough.

What we need is a better approach to the way that we manage the total landscape. So I don't believe that a question like that has a single simple answer. It all depends on how we're treating the rest of the environment overall.   **JEFF MCNEELY**

What does wilderness do for us?

People depend on many so-called wilderness areas for their supplies of food, for their fresh water, for their ability to go into the forest and harvest timber and fibres for their lifestyle. Of course, many people are making use of wilderness these days for recreation, and there's an enormous industry built up around tourism. So it's both an intrinsic cultural affinity with wilderness and a very practical basis on which people's lives are dependent on many of these wilderness areas.

We find that wilderness areas in particular have an important role to play in global regulation of the planet in terms of climate regulation and water flow. So, for example, the polar regions are particularly important in reflecting solar radiation back to the atmosphere and helping in the regulation of global climate. The same is true with deserts. Tundra systems are particularly important in world-climate regulation, as they have a role to play in the sequestration, or locking up, of carbon in the planet. As tundra systems are increasingly being affected by climate change, we're finding they're drying out in many parts of the world, and that's leading to a release of carbon into the atmosphere.   **NEVILLE ASH**

If Earth was without life it would be, like Mars or Venus, a planet-sized desert with a carbon dioxide atmosphere. Life has kept the Earth watered since it began over 3 billion years ago. Gaia is the name given to the great self-regulating system that has kept the Earth habitable, and Gaia theory sees life evolving not alone but tightly coupled with the air the oceans and the surface rocks.

Wilderness is more than important – it's vital. The natural ecosystems of the Earth are what keep the climate and the composition of the atmosphere and the oceans just right for life, and it's been happening like that through the great system Gaia for nearly a quarter of the age of the universe. We've been foolish enough to take away wilderness to use as farmland to feed ourselves and for wood to build our homes and make furniture, and when we take it away we are damaging the ability of the Earth to regulate itself. It's much more important, I think, to sustain wilderness around the Earth and try and get it to grow back than it is to avoid emissions of carbon dioxide and other gases, which attract most of the attention.

JAMES LOVELOCK

We all are inclined to believe that the ocean is for all practical purposes a true wilderness and infinite. The truth is that it is finite. The ocean is the thinnest imaginable film stretched taut, so to speak, across the surface of the Earth. It is not capable of continuing to receive everything we dump into it. But unfortunately, because the ocean is downhill from everything on Earth, everything that can be moved by water or wind or by any means at all eventually ends up in the ocean. And that means that we really need to pay attention to the oceans of the world or we will pay the price. It's no longer just 'Oh wouldn't it be nice to have clean oceans.' We're about to lose access to one of our principal sources of animal protein. I believe that humanity is about to lose access to fish from the sea because the sea is becoming too polluted for the fish to be clean enough to eat safely. Nearly two billion people depend as their principal source of animal protein on seafood. If we lose access to seafood in this way, you could say that would probably be the biggest public-health threat humanity has ever faced.

Everybody has always said the solution to pollution is dilution, so that when toxic substances get into the ocean they are hugely diluted down and become harmless. And that's quite right – that happens. But then a totally insidious thing also happens: they get picked up in the oils of plankton, particularly of diatoms – those microscopic, single-celled plants of which the ocean

it's no longer just 'Oh wouldn't it be nice to have clean oceans.' We're about to lose access to one of our principal sources of animal protein

is composed. If you are eating an animal like a swordfish, for example, and that animal lives at about the sixth level of the food pyramid, it means that the flesh of the swordfish contains a million times as much contaminants as was in the water around the fish. So if you ate a pound of swordfish, for example, you would be eating all of the pollutants that had been collected by a million pounds (that's 500 tons) of diatoms. That's a real problem.

There's a secondary problem that affects us because we're mammals. Any woman of childbearing age, if she's nursing her infant – that tenderest of all mammalian acts – what she is actually doing is dumping her lifetime's accumulation of fat-soluble pollutants into that infant. If her milk was in containers other than her breasts, she would not be allowed to take it across a state line. It's too polluted. That's something people have to concern themselves with. Our species can dodge that bullet by simply feeding formula to our children – but that is not an option for a whale. So the only conclusion you can draw is that these pollutants, as they build higher, are going to bring species to extinction. That's a problem we ought to be concerned with.   **ROGER PAYNE**

One of the biggest values of wilderness is the fact that it provides enormous ecosystem services for the planet – simple watershed protection, the hydrological cycles, for example. About 20 per cent of the world's water runs through Amazonia. If you cut down that forest, we don't know exactly what the impacts are going to be, but you can be sure that there are going to be huge climatic impacts around the world.

RUSSELL MITTERMEIER

When habitats are changed, the services or the benefits they deliver to people can change very dramatically. In some cases, it's for the benefit of people: where we've converted systems into agricultural areas, that has been at the benefit of many people for the increased production of food. But, in fact, when we're doing that, we're also losing some of the benefits which people have had before. So, for example, mangrove systems around the world are being reduced in extent, often to make way for aquaculture systems. And whilst the aquaculture system can provide enormous private gains to the individuals involved in aquaculture farming – often for shrimp for the tables in Europe and North America – the local people are then deprived of the previous benefits they derived from the mangrove system in terms of the nursery functions of the mangrove for fisheries, in terms of the coastal erosion and protection functions of the mangroves, in terms of the fuel wood and the other timber resources coming from the mangrove. The short-term gains are often much smaller than the longer-term benefits derived from a particular natural system to a wider range of individuals.

while the aquaculture system can provide enormous private gains to the individuals involved in aquaculture farming … the local people are then deprived of the previous benefits they derived from the mangrove

In many cases it's not clear that the ecosystem might have changed. It's not been converted, it still looks fairly intact, but we're losing species from within the ecosystem, which is having a very dramatic change on the way in which the system is able to provide benefits to people. For example, forest systems may look like intact forests, but they may have been degraded because they've lost particular species that are harvested for food. They may have lost particularly important timber species. So changes to the composition of a particular ecosystem as well as the extent of the habitat are also important. **NEVILLE ASH**

What about medicinal plants?

People argue that 25 to 50 per cent of modern medicines owe their origin to plants. Due to historical developments, most of these have come from temperate plants, but the diversity of the tropical rainforest is probably ten times that of temperate forests, which means there are ten times more medicinal species waiting to be analysed and waiting to yield new drugs for diseases we may not even know yet. **JAMES A. DUKE**

> there is a much greater possibility of finding remarkable active chemicals in rainforest ... than probably anywhere else on the planet

The obvious practical value of some of the yet-to-be-discovered plants in the rainforest is already quite clear. It is a curious feature of rainforest plants that, because of the enormous complexity of the relations that the plants have with each other and with their insects, they have had to evolve an amazing bio-chemistry of defence chemicals against insects, or transmitters which attract one group of insects and put off another group. So there is a much greater possibility of finding remarkable active chemicals in rainforest – in canopies, especially – than probably anywhere else on the planet, and these may well be useful to humans, as drugs, as ways of making polymers and materials, as foods and, more frivolously, as perfumes.

RICHARD MABEY

The Madagascar periwinkle is one of four herbs that I call billion-dollar herbs. It's probably been 50 years since it was discovered, quite by accident, that it wiped out white blood corpuscles. Researchers were studying it for diabetes, and their rats died. But their rats died from a lack of white corpuscles, and then the light bulb went on, and they realized that it would be good for wiping up the abnormal white blood corpuscles produced by leukaemia. The Madagascar periwinkle contains over 500 named alkaloids, but the two most important are vincristine and vinblastine, which are sold pharmacologically pure and used as prescription drugs. Since then, for at least 50 years, the drugs vincristine and vinblastine have been selling for roughly $100 million a year. That's why I call it a billion-dollar drug plant.

JAMES DUKE

What is the market value of wilderness?

Many of those ecosystem services are what you might call public goods. They're not things that people can exclude others benefiting from, and one person's use of those goods doesn't affect other people's use of those goods. Therefore, markets don't automatically arise for those goods and services, and like all public goods, you need other ways of incorporating their value. One way of doing that is to try to look at how those systems affect human welfare in various ways, and there are a whole range of techniques that one might use for that.

For coral reefs, one might look at the benefits that are derived from people diving on coral reefs and experiencing the recreational opportunities. One might also look at the habitat that reefs provide for fish that are caught and provide food. One might look at the effects of coral reefs in terms of sequestering carbon – taking carbon dioxide out of the atmosphere and therefore keeping the climate stable. So there is a whole range of benefits, each one of which might have a different technique that one would use for quantifying it. But when you pull all those things together, you get very large numbers in terms of the dollar value per hectare of coral reefs – in the order of thousands of dollars per hectare – and those numbers are almost certainly underestimates, because we're always going to leave certain services out that are harder to quantify.

Why is this important? The conventional economic view of natural ecosystems is that they are luxury goods, things that we can afford to do without, but in fact nothing could be further from the truth.

Ecological systems are life-support systems – they support our welfare in very critical ways that other systems can't substitute. So we want to bring that information into the decision-making process, where a lot of our decisions are made on the basis of economics and relative costs and benefits. If we fail to express those services in units that are comparable, then the assumption is that those values are zero. They get ignored. So it's a way to bring those

the conventional economic view of natural ecosystems is that they are luxury goods, things that we can afford to do without, but in fact nothing could be further from the truth

> we've estimated that the total value of all ecosystem services far exceeds the big global GDP

services onto the table to say, 'these are important, these are critical to our welfare, broadly conceived.' Even though they're not marketed in the conventional way – they're not part of the market exchange system – they are equally if not more valuable than all of the marketed services that exist on the planet today. We've estimated that the total value of all ecosystem services far exceeds the big global GDP. If one's talking about human welfare, then ecosystems and their services are at least as important – probably far more important – than the conventional economy.   **ROBERT COSTANZA**

One of the reasons that biodiversity and ecosystems around the world are being degraded is that their true values are not recognized in current economic systems. So it is useful to try to put some kind of valuation on ecosystems.

It is possible in many places to put a dollar value on the benefits which we're deriving from them. There are lots of case studies where we can look at the actual dollar values coming from a particular wetland or a particular forest, but they're often very case or site specific, and it's very difficult then to broaden those up from a case study to a regional, national or global level.   **NEVILLE ASH**

Valuing ecosystems raises of course the fact that value is one of those very extensive English words stretching from deep emotional attachments to simple cost-accounting. To value an ecosystem, one can do it at either end of the scale. For myself, being an impractical person, I would prefer us to begin by valuing ecosystems just because they are there, because both the individual organisms that comprise them and the astonishing complexity by which they've been connected are intrinsically beautiful and worthwhile, certainly as worthwhile as we are. But that, in the real world, doesn't pull weight at the moment. I wish it did.

Valuing ecosystems economically is being done more and more at the moment. It runs the danger of trivialization – of oversimplifying complicated systems into simple ones and the necessity of ignoring certain vital things that we may not even know are vital yet – simply to get the equation manageable. But as a working idea to get people's imaginations moving, I think it's useful.

James Lovelock has done a cost-accounting of the value of the oxygen from the Amazonian rainforests and what it might mean if the rest of the world were to pay Brazil for the oxygen it imports, and it is a very considerable sum of money, as you might imagine. And to inject that sort of thinking, even if you haven't got a hope in hell of it actually being realized as an economic transaction, is a way of reshaping people's thinking to understand that economic transactions are also ecological. The air that we, as it were, metaphorically buy from Brazil is the air the rest of the world needs. The costing of it underlines the ecological importance.

RICHARD MABEY

I think if putting monetary value on ecosystems means a way of saying we can, as it were, pay for them, can compensate for their loss, then we'd better be very careful about that. It's a very functionalist, very narrow view. What is more important is that economists are simply saying environmental cost is real cost. It's not just what they call an externality. It's not simply an indifferent consequence on the edge of what you're actually doing. It's somehow intrinsic to the economic activity you're undertaking. Bringing together the issues of economy and ecology seems to me one of the great imperatives. This is not to reduce ecology to economy but in a sense almost the other way round – to insist on what has often been said, the fact that the economy is wholly a subsidiary of the environment.**ROWAN WILLIAMS, ARCHBISHOP OF CANTERBURY**

I think the trend towards putting a value on ecosystems is critically important, because we need to recognize increasingly that ecosystems are the essential underpinnings of our economy. And we will only build the protection of those ecosystems into our own development if we recognize their economic value.

JAMES LEAPE

The reason that people are working so diligently to put an economic value on ecosystem services is that we're at a moment in human history when economic factors are driving human behaviour, at least at the policy-making level. People want to know what's in it for me? How much is it worth? And so the conservation movement, which has tended to be an ethical movement, that has assumed that nature is worth conserving for itself, has also started to look much more carefully at the economic values of conservation and of biodiversity. And we're finding surprising things about how valuable the ecosystems of the world are, for the services they deliver to people.

For conservationists, conserving biodiversity is a good idea, period. But there also are good economic reasons for conservation. If you harvest a resource in a sustainable way, you will have it forever into the future. If you overexploit that resource, then you are certain to lose it at some point in the future. The cod fishery in Canada was so heavily overfished that it collapsed. Fishing stopped, but the cod have not come back. This to me is a tragic story, and had we been able to put a better economic value on the costs of overexploitation at an earlier time in the cycle, we may have been able to convince the fisheries officials not to allow fishing at such a high level. If we're going to convince the decision-makers, they need cash values so that they can take the trade-offs to the parliamentarians and can present economic reality to the public, who often seem to understand monetary values better than they do ethical values.

JEFF MCNEELY

I think it is inevitable that we're going to have to put a market price, a money value on more and more aspects of the environment, because we live in a monetized world. The only thing that seems to give people a signal of value is a pound sign or a dollar sign. Now, in that world, trying to persuade people that nature is above any valuation and beyond price and all the rest of it, simply doesn't wash. We've gone too far philosophically for that to work any longer. So in certain instances, putting a money value on something can make all the difference.

If one takes reefs, for instance, think in terms of the productivity of that area, the biological diversity, the value to local communities of that place as a breeding ground for fish, for tourism and so on: stick a money value on it, and then say to people, 'How smart do you think you're going to be if you destroy that today for a fraction of the ongoing economic value of that asset over years and years?' That may make a difference in the minds of some decision-makers who think that short-term liquidation of natural assets is still the answer, when, in fact, long-term management of those assets gives a very much better economic return.

I've been hugely impressed by those economists who do these incredible calculations about how much it would cost us to do something if nature didn't do it for us for free. So you get these sort of multi-billion-dollar assessments of what would happen if bees and other insects stopped pollinating for us – which is the one I really like, because nobody thinks very much about pollination as a gift from nature! But if they all stopped doing it, they just went on strike, and we had to do it by human intervention, by man-made means, you look at the price tag for that and it's x hundred billion dollars or whatever. So our entire productive food enterprise is subsidized by nature. It's only when you shove that price sign under some people's eyes that they think, 'Maybe this natural world is a bit more useful to us than we thought it was.' Then tot up all these other ecosystem services, and you get this huge sum of money, which of course isn't a proper calculation, but it is a means of reminding people of the degree to which we are still completely

how smart do you think you're going to be if you destroy that today for a fraction of the ongoing economic value of that asset over years and years?

we've never learned how to do sustainable-yield management in all the history of mankind

dependent on the natural world, not just aesthetically and spiritually but completely dependent economically for the services it provides for us.

Why do we have to make that transition? At the moment, we go on thinking we're smart enough to manage natural systems, to maximize the sustainable yield from them. We have this illusion that we're into sustainable asset-management. So here's a fishery. We'll manage it just to get the perfect amount of product off it every year. Here's a forest. We'll manage it for this purpose.

We never get it right. We've never learned how to do sustainable-yield management at all in the history of humankind. So as long as we go on perpetuating that fantasy about sustainable management of that sort, we are going to continue to hit the buffers when it comes to handling nature's wealth in a more responsible way. So we need a bigger ethic. We need a less money-based ethic to get the balance into our understanding of what the natural world is really doing for us.

JONATHON PORRITT

The problem here is that we have to put a money value on things in today's world to persuade people that they're valuable and important. But in so doing, we're betraying the cause that we stand for. We're saying the only reason why you should care about the world is because it's of financial value to us. And once we are coopted by that monetization process, by turning everything into a hard-edged dollar value, then we've lost it. So keeping that balance between using the tools and the metrics of a market-based economy and keeping the integrity and ethics of our approach properly based, properly grounded, that is a really big challenge. But it's a challenge that we've got to rise to.

I'm not worried about putting an economic value on ecosystem services – I think it's absolutely essential. If we don't increasingly put value on the services provided by nature, it's going to be difficult to justify protecting them. We want to protect for aesthetic and spiritual and moral reasons, but in many developing countries, where the vast majority of biodiversity exists and where the bulk of the wilderness areas exist, if we don't come up with some economic rationale for protecting these areas, then ultimately it's going to be a real uphill battle to convince governments to conserve them.

I don't see it as selling out in any way, I really think it's a great opportunity for us, because without these ecosystem services, we as a species worldwide – developing country, developed country, whatever – are going to be in serious trouble.

There are some very innovative approaches being developed now. For instance, Costa Rica has come up with this concept of forests as water factories, and they're actually paying farmers who are letting their pastureland go back into forest for the water services that are being provided by these forests. This is something that we'd like to see developed in many other countries around the world, because I think it's going to be a real boon for nature conservation in general.

RUSSELL MITTERMEIER

Why do poor people decide to liquidate a forest? Actually, they often don't decide that. Some big company tells them: 'Liquidate it. We're going to give you some money.' So that's the incentive, ultimately. It works if the only value those trees have is as a lumber product.

Now, if we can start understanding, quantifying and then building into our economic systems the other values that forest might provide, then what we're doing is balancing that equation a little bit better. I personally believe – at least, in many instances – that if we balance out that equation, then there will be

Costa Rica has come up with this concept of forests as water factories, and they're actually paying farmers who are letting their pastureland go back into forest for the water services that are being provided by these forests strong incentives for local people not to liquidate that asset, because that asset is worth more as it's standing right now than lopped off in a bank, earning interest. But it has to be worth something in terms of dollars in their pockets. It's not going to be worth something as an intellectual exercise.

So take trees, for example. Look at all the services they can provide, of course, like lumber. Now that's the one that you usually use for liquidation. They can provide some ecotourism opportunities if you get the right kind of market. They can provide some recreational opportunities if you can provide the market. Carbon – as a sink for carbon dioxide, to mitigate against climate change. Fresh water, as a provider and a protector of watersheds. Security as in a buffer from landslides and so on. It's no coincidence that the Philippines is one of the most deforested countries in Asia and also the country that suffers the largest number of landslides.

So no matter how much money you have, if the whole hillside falls on your head, it sort of makes the point moot. So once you start pricing all of those services in there – and you can build those prices for it – it can really translate into real dollars for people. Then it seems the liquidation pressure won't be so enticing. **M. SANJAYAN**

If we don't demonstrate that wilderness areas and other natural areas have an economic value, a very real value to global society, we run the risk of them being liquidated for other short-term reasons. We really need to come up with a whole range of different justifications, economic justifications for protecting them.

My principal objective is to protect them because they're very special – the aesthetic, the moral reasons for doing so. But we need to be practical as well and come up with very real economic arguments that demonstrate that they have value to global society. Otherwise, the environment in general is always going to be an afterthought in global and national planning. We have to make the environment the fundamental underpinning of sustainable development and long-term human survival, and this is one of the best ways we can do it.

RUSSELL MITTERMEIER

we have to make the environment the fundamental underpinning of ... long-term human survival

We need to value the services that ecosystems are providing to us. Right now we tend to not put any value on them at all, and so it's very easy to drain or fill a wetland and put in a shopping mall, because we tend to attribute zero value to the wetland. And so I think – to the extent that we begin to give it a monetary value – we at least provide the signal that the wetland is worth something and we should be careful about whether we decide to put that land to another use.

The danger I see in putting a monetary value on particular ecosystems is that then it's almost impossible to come up with a number that really fully takes into account the total value. We can put some value on the purification services of a wetland. What would it cost, if we lost that wetland, to purify that water with a treatment plant?

Well, you can calculate that and compare the two and make some reasonable estimate. But for many services – cultural values, recreational values, aesthetic values, the ethical values attributed to safeguarding the life of species that are endangered – these things are very hard to quantify monetarily. So valuation is a tool we can use, but we shouldn't make it the determining factor in most decisions.

SANDRA POSTEL

Can we weigh the value of fossil fuels against that of wilderness?

There are many frontier regions, wilderness regions, that are still under threat because of our hunger to get more fossil fuels out of the ground – from Alaska to central Asia, to the rainforests of the Amazon.

the oil they're going to get out of there is just a few months' worth of supply for the US. Surely the wiser route is towards fuel efficiency and alternatives

Companies are looking for new fuel sources to feed this global insatiable demand for oil and gas in particular. One of the regions is Alaska, including protected areas like the Arctic National Wildlife Refuge [ANWR], where companies are now being granted permission by the administration of George W. Bush to go into previously protected areas to get out the oil. Now, that isn't only going to cause problems for the local wildlife and indigenous inhabitants, it's obviously going to fuel climate-change. And the oil they're going to get out of there is just a few months' worth of supply for the US. Surely the wiser route is towards fuel efficiency and alternatives rather than trying to get more of this stuff out of the ground?

One of the paradoxes with the dwindling nature of oil and gas supplies is that exploration is becoming more aggressive. You may have thought that, as the price went up for oil and gas, people would have invested in alternatives. Some of that is happening, but people are actually putting more and more resources into finding the remaining oil and gas, even in areas where it previously would have been too expensive to drill. Even in Alaska, where conditions are very difficult, the rising price of oil means it's economic to go in there.   **TONY JUNIPER**

Tundra's important because it's more than just an ecosystem. It is a whole concatenation of ecosystems, what we call a biome. It is absolutely unique in its climatic regime of course, in its soil, but also in the fauna and the flora that has taken countless tens of millions of years to evolve in its present state.

Some people say that it's empty. They don't know the tundra. There are forms of life there in great profusion: lichens, for example, and, of course, bird life, including that which comes north to the high Arctic to breed and feed during the summer season: mammals and insects of great abundance that are found nowhere else on Earth. If you think the tundra is empty, except maybe for some distant herd of caribou, you haven't learned how to look yet. It's also unique because it's among those areas that have been too forbidding for human beings to mess up considerably. So we have a large part of the world that is in a pristine condition. It's not a part of the world that people particularly love living in, anyway, and it seems almost criminal not to leave it as a wilderness area for the Earth as a whole. **E.O. WILSON**

if you think the tundra is empty, except maybe for some distant herd of caribou, you haven't learned how to look

We should absolutely be drilling for oil in ANWR. It's the most promising reserve in the United States that we have right now. You're talking an area that's 2000 acres out of over 19 million acres [800 hectares out of over 7.6 million hectares]. Potentially 10.4 billion barrels of oil are there, and that's the mean estimate. So we should absolutely be drilling for oil in ANWR. We can do it in an environmentally safe manner. It's technological development. We have the ability to drill laterally now – that is, go straight down beneath the Earth's surface and actually branch out sideways to extract oil, rather than setting up a derrick on every single piece of property. The roads and the landing strips that would be needed to transport the infrastructure in and out of ANWR would be made of ice. In the spring, the ice melts and there's no trace of the roads. When the ice forms again, the roads are built and we go about our business again. There is absolutely no reason that we shouldn't be drilling for oil in ANWR, from an environmental standpoint or an energy standpoint.

A lot of the environmental arguments that surrounded the Alaska pipeline said that it would have a detrimental effect on the caribou population, when in reality – according to reports that are now pretty generally accepted – the pipeline has actually been beneficial to the caribou in some instances, because it provides warmth. They're attracted to the pipeline, they mate near the pipeline, and the population has increased I believe sixfold since the pipeline was created. So again these are a lot of the same tired arguments that we've heard from those who are trying to scare people away from necessary energy development that really doesn't harm the environment. **PEYTON KNIGHT**

One of the problems with managing the environment in a more sustainable way is that we don't know what our impacts are going to be. There's a lot of uncertainty about our activities. A way of solving that problem is to shift the burden of that uncertainty from the public to the parties that stand to gain. It's just an additional cost that private parties and private companies are not currently bearing. One could require assurance bonds to be posted whenever a potentially risky environmental activity was undertaken, so that the risk would be borne by the parties that stand to gain from that activity.

An example would be exploration for oil in ANWR, where the oil companies contend that the environmental damages would be minimal, but there's a potential risk there. The real question is, who bears that risk? If we just say: 'Go ahead and drill and try to be careful,' well, that's one thing. But if we said: 'Post a bond large enough to cover the worst-case damages, and you can recover that bond if and when those damages are shown to be less,' then that's a whole different affair as far as the company is concerned. They would be much more careful. They would bear the financial burden of that risk.

We use this kind of system all the time in construction, for example, when contractors are required to post the bond large enough to cover the damages that might occur if the building falls down. That does lead them to be much more careful about how they run the construction operation and prevents the sort of fly-by-night operators from coming in and then skipping town when something goes wrong. So I think we have the same sort of situation with environmental protection. We want those parties that are affecting the environment and the ecosystem services and public goods to be financially responsible, and we want assurance that that's the case. **ROBERT COSTANZA**

As an American citizen, I really would rather not see us drilling in ANWR, because I think, as the richest country on Earth, we should be able to set aside certain areas as being pristine and worthy of preservation in their own right. So I very much hope that the ANWR drilling never actually takes place. Whether or not it's done carefully and whether it's going to have a huge impact is very much discussed. Certainly it's going to have some impact on migration routes and breeding for the caribou in that part of the north. But I don't know that we'll see species extinctions as you would get in a tropical forest if you engaged in mining or deforestation activities. But I would really like to see some parts of the United States maintained in pristine condition, and I don't think there's real economic justification for going in there and drilling oil.

My personal opinion is that it's not going to resolve our oil issues. We would be much better off just engaging in more serious conservation, better energy use, looking at a whole range of alternatives. Simply drilling for oil in one of the last wilderness blocks in our country is foolish, given the range of other options that are out there. I would be very sad and actually embarrassed as an American were it to take place.

RUSSELL MITTERMEIER

To open ANWR to exploration and drilling would not be criminal, but it's the closest thing I can imagine to being criminal. It is quite unneeded, really, in terms of what it can provide as new energy to our gas-guzzling American public. And what would be lost forever, in the dwindling world of wilderness, to America and to the world, would be immense – almost beyond measure. So what you're doing, in suggesting that it be opened, is to put on one side of the scale a relatively trivial amount of economic short-term gain, and on the other side, something that will be valued with increasing magnitude for all time to come. **E.O. WILSON**

6

Growing Population on a Limited Earth

The Earth's human population has grown from a billion in 1800 to 6.5 billion today, and it's predicted to continue rising to more than 9 billion by 2050. What impact do so many of a single, very exploitative species have on the planet, what is the planet's limit, and have we already reached it? Just how many people can the Earth really be expected to support?

Population is the whole problem, really. Malthus, a philosopher 200 years ago, was worried about the number of people on the Earth then. In his time there were about a billion, and he said there would be trouble if we went on reproducing. And he was dead right. If we'd listened to him and stopped then, we wouldn't be in the problem we're in now.

With just a billion people, we could do almost anything, and it wouldn't harm the planet – and there would be no further problems. But at 6 billion and growing, the planet just can't cope. We take too much at our current style of living. I'm not talking just about the West, I'm talking about our farming style of living. Once you start herding animals, that's a terribly inefficient way of getting food. You use 20 times as much land as you would if you stayed vegetarian or hunter-gatherer.

So, we're all in it – West *and* undeveloped world.   **JAMES LOVELOCK**

I think the rate at which populations are now growing is a very serious issue. Clearly we do live in a limited environment. I wouldn't like to push the problem off onto overpopulation, in the way that has sometimes been fashionable. People usually say, 'Well, the real problem about the environment is that there are too many people in Africa and India.' In other words, it's not about us. Overpopulation has to be seen as a global issue, not just something that we can tell other people to do something about – or, indeed, buy into some of the vile and unjust methods of population-control that have occasionally cropped up.

ROWAN WILLIAMS, ARCHBISHOP OF CANTERBURY

The population story is phenomenal. In around 1800, there were a billion of us – and the demographers say that's as many human beings as had ever existed since we evolved, about 160,000 years ago in what is now Ethiopia. By 1960 there were 3 billion of us. Now there are 6 billion, and there's going to be 9 billion by 2020 to 2030, and that's inevitable.

I think the growth of human population is the fundamental explanation of the massive growing strain on the environmental resources of the world. Lots of people say, 'Well, let's not have so many people,' but who's going to kill whom? You can't kill people – the only way is to accept. If you take Bangladesh, say, the largest, least developed country in the world – it has about 130 million people. More and more girls are going to school, contraception is available and used, and family size is declining quite rapidly. But it's a very young country. So, its population is going to increase by 50 per cent over the next 30 years because just those young couples will have their few children. Then it will stabilize. So we're going to 9 billion. However, 90 per cent of the new people will be born in the poorest countries, and if we don't manage things differently, there's going to be chaos, famine and suffering.

CLARE SHORT

> the growth of human population is the fundamental explanation of the massive growing strain on the environmental resources of the world

The number one problem for conservation, of course, is population growth worldwide, and it's particularly strong here in Africa, because we're the last continent to undergo what's called the demographic transition. Asia, Latin America – their population rates have slowed down to a point closer to what we're used to in Europe and North America. But in Africa, family size is still very large. Economic security is still very low – so there's an incentive for people to have very large families, and these are families that require basic natural resources for their subsistence. So the impact of people on the natural world is still growing quite strikingly here. **CRAIG PACKER**

There is no question that human numbers, multiplied by each individual's footprint on the planet, is the driver of destruction of habitats around the world. But the second part of that equation is critical: it is how we live on the planet, not just our total numbers that really makes the essential difference.

If we all live on this planet the way Americans currently live, that is, if we have the footprint that an average American currently has, we would need three planets to support the Earth's current population. So that consumption level – that footprint – is crucial. **JAMES LEAPE**

it's not simply an issue of the number of people. It's the number of people and to what degree can they purchase and use energy and biological and other natural resources, such as water, etc

Many people try to blame population growth as the major threat to our ecosystems. I personally don't agree. The population of the world today is just over 6 billion people, and it's likely to increase to between 8 and 10 billion people by 2050 – about a 50 per cent increase. Over that same time frame, the global annual economy is likely to increase by a factor of four, from around $35 to $40 trillion today to nearly $150 trillion by 2050. The threat to the environment is a combination of the number of people and their consumption patterns, with consumption patterns being driven largely by economic wealth. Therefore, it's not simply an issue of the number of people. It's the number of people and to what degree can they purchase and use energy and biological and other natural resources such as water, etc.

I would argue the bigger threat to ecological systems is the growth in our economy and the way we use our wealth. It's a multitude of factors.

ROBERT WATSON

The population has quadrupled from something like 1.6 billion at the turn of the twentieth century to about 6 billion at the end of it. However, the amount of consumption has increased by a factor of 16. That surely is not sustainable, and the growth was utterly dependent on a source of energy that is non-renewable, namely oil. If we consider all the ways that oil has supported the increase in human population and recognize that oil is no longer going to be nearly as freely available, we can expect a serious population crunch at some point in the foreseeable future.

JEFF MCNEELY

I think the increase in the human population is a very serious threat. Almost all the ills that are afflicting the planet would be reduced if there were fewer people. The concentration of individuals of this one species, *Homo sapiens*, has produced a huge shift in the balance of things. People say, 'Look at the Indians of the Amazon. What wonderful ecologists they are. They live in harmony with nature.' The fact is that there are a tiny number of them living in a very considerable area. If you took Amazonian Indians, or anybody, and made them live in concentrations that are common in Western Europe and in big cities, you would find that they, too, would create all the ecological and sociological problems that afflict our citites. It's not a simple equation, because Americans, who are materially wealthy, are using much more than Africans, who are not. So, there are complications, but by and large, the size of the population is a very powerful element in nearly all our problems.

DAVID ATTENBOROUGH

One thing that's always worried me about the environment movement for the last 30 years, is environmentalists' inability to get their heads around the importance of population. I find it staggering that that is still downgraded as an issue. There's a sense it's somehow politically incorrect to talk about population. But the issue of population lies absolutely at the heart of the destruction of the natural world today. If we had to find a way of creating a sustainable future for a billion people, I can assure you it would be a great deal simpler and a lot better for the natural world than trying to find a solution for 6 billion people, let alone 9 billion people. So ignoring population strikes me as the biggest own-goal that the environment movement has ever scored against itself, and it really concerns me that that has meant politicians can get away with paying zero attention to probably the most important issue of our time.

There are good reasons why people aren't very good at dealing with population, but they're not good enough to justify the inaction, the indifference. Because if you look at the world today, there is a fantastically good story to be told about population – which is when countries get on top of family planning, learn how to provide that magic combination of literacy and better health care for women and girls and to provide access to a range of contraceptives. That's what good family planning is all about. There need be no coercion involved, no intrusions into human rights, none of the cruelty that has happened in some countries. This can be done by focusing on good models of development and particularly by focusing on women-centred development in male-dominated cultures. Why that hasn't been part of our progressive approach to the environment for all these years, I still honestly do find very difficult to understand.   **JONATHON PORRITT**

Until fairly recently a great many people thought, 'Well, you might as well live for today – make the most of it – because the human population is exploding. It's going to destroy all the natural part of the world, it's going to eat up our resources and it's going to be downhill all the way from here on, baby.' That's been a very common feeling. It turns out that, due to a providential quality of human nature, that [scenario] is not necessarily true. When women are given any kind of freedom, and particularly economic freedom, and their choice on how to make money and how to run their lives, including their reproductive lives, the fertility rate plummets. It's plummeted from about six children per woman around the middle of the last century, to about three children per woman today, and it's coming on down. It's come down below break-even point in all of the European countries.

In other parts of the world – in Asia for example, where there is some degree of women's freedom to choose – it comes down, too. The United Nations has therefore estimated that, if trends continue, we can expect to see the human population peak by the end of the century to roughly 9 billion people. That's somewhere around 40 per cent more than we have.

Now, we can handle another 40 per cent. We can feed them. And with sane environmental and conservation practices, we can actually save most of the remaining wildernesses and natural world and biodiversity. It can be done. There is a catch, however, that we have to face up to, which is that per capita consumption is going up. People are individually consuming more and more. So the question then is no longer simply population control but also something that is entirely consistent with improving individual human welfare anyway, and that is to improve the quality of life of people all around the world while reducing their per-capita material and energy consumption.

Now, if that sounds like a paradox, I disagree. It can be done. We've been talking now for many years about how to reduce energy consumption with alternative sources, how to grow more food in the areas that are already under cultivation. We can handle this as we go through this bottleneck that we are now in, with little damage to ourselves and to nature and end up with a better quality of life, carrying through as much of the natural world that we inherited as we can at the end of it. Because we are the only species that can actually understand what it's doing, can know its history, can project into its future and can figure out what happens if it overconsumes or overexploits the natural environment. **E.O. WILSON**

> we are the only species that can actually understand what it's doing, can know its history, can project into its future and can figure out what happens if it overconsumes or overexploits the natural environment

It's clear that we need to limit the number of people in the world. We should do it, though, in a culturally acceptable manner. In my opinion, the combination of education of girls and the empowerment of women typically tends to lead to smaller family sizes. This can be combined with culturally acceptable forms of contraception. At the same time, economic growth is required to lift a significant number of people out of poverty – half the world's population lives on less than two dollars a day. This is totally and utterly unacceptable. We need economic growth and, in particular, we need pro-poor economic growth. We then need to make sure that, as the demand for energy increases, it is environmentally friendly, with respect to the Earth's climate, the local environment and water resources. As we use biological resources, the question is how do we make sure that we have the most efficient use of them? As the world's economy grows, the threat to the environment grows, but that's inevitable, in my opinion. The challenge for us, then, is how to use our resources in the most sustainable manner possible. **ROBERT WATSON**

We are damaging ourselves as human beings because we are destroying the condition of life on Earth. UNEP, the United Nations Environment Programme, is meant to protect the environment *and* protect humans, because at the end of the day, we are not protecting species for their beauty. We are protecting species for their use for humans – for our food, for our shelter, for our clothes and for other purposes. And UNEP is trying to demonstrate that we can continue to grow and to respond to our needs as human beings

the approach that we have to nature and our relations with natural resources need to change

while protecting the environment. We are not doomed to grow while destroying the environment. It's a huge contradiction, I agree, but it's something that we have to do – we have to respond to our needs, our growing needs, at the same time protecting the only planet that we have.

I believe sincerely that the crux of the issue is our attitude towards resources. The approach that we have to nature and our relations with natural resources need to change. If we follow the same pattern of lifestyle of the US citizen, we need five planets. The European Union has recognized that, in order to sustain the same lifestyle, Europeans need two Europe territories, because they are overconsuming the services of the territory. It's not sustainable because now everyone on Earth, including what we call the emerging countries, countries like China and India, aspire to have the same lifestyle. And this cannot be done. So we need to rethink our relations with resources, with Mother Nature.

AHMED DJOGHLAF

I think we have to change our conception of what the economy is and what the economy is for. The conventional view is that the economy is there to produce goods and services, and the more we produce and consume, the better off we'll be. But there's a lot of evidence to show that's not really the case. Consumption of goods and services only improves people's sense of satisfaction up to a fairly low threshold, beyond which it becomes counterproductive in terms of their long-term well-being. So, the economy really should be for producing sustainable human well-being – welfare – and that's a very complex function that involves natural capital and ecosystem services, social capital and people's

> there's a lot of psychological evidence that people who are too focused on material consumption are also people with higher rates of both mental and physical illnesses

interactions with other people, their families and their friends and human capital – their health, their education, etc, as well as the conventional consumption of goods and services.

I could add one thing to that. There's a lot of psychological evidence that people who are too focused on material consumption are also people with higher rates of both mental and physical illnesses. Our focus on consumption is a form of psychological junk food. It's something that makes us feel good temporarily, but in the end it makes us unhealthy. It's not a sacrifice. It's something that would actually improve welfare from the status quo. Our current path is not sustainable, but it's also not desirable. So how do we create a more sustainable and desirable future? Well there are a lot of positive things happening these days, including the country of Bhutan having recently declared that its national policy goal is gross national happiness, rather than gross national product. There are other countries beginning to take on board more of these ideas – towards the vision of improving quality of life, not just increasing consumption and standard of living. I think that's the bottom line. We can consume less and be better off than we are.   **ROBERT COSTANZA**

What are some of the impacts of increasing population?

With an increasing human population, it's inevitable that there are going to be more and more trade-offs to make between the ways in which we manage the environment. For example, about 30 per cent of the terrestrial surface of the Earth is now under agricultural systems. We're going to need more food to feed more mouths; we're going to need more living spaces; we're going to need more commodities, more resources. And they're going to have to be found from the natural world. If we convert an area of wilderness into agricultural land, we're going to increase the production of food, and that's important, because we need more food to feed more mouths now and into the future. But the reality is, when we cut down or convert wilderness to agricultural lands, we're making a trade-off. We're benefiting from the increased food production, but we're losing some of the benefits of that land in terms of the vast array of other services it would offer. **NEVILLE ASH**

Nature has dealt us a very difficult hand when it comes to water. Where do you want to grow crops? You want to grow crops where it's sunny and where it's warm, and those are the places that don't have as much rainfall. So what we need to do is irrigate, and we need to irrigate in exactly those places where rainfall is scarce and, therefore, water is scarce. Irrigation is a big intrusion in the natural water cycle. We get 40 per cent of our food from irrigated land, even though that land makes up less than 20 per cent of the whole cropland base. Seventy per cent of all the water we take out of rivers, lakes and aquifers goes to irrigation. So it consumes the lion's share of the water that we're taking out of the natural world.

A key thing, it seems to me, as population increases, is that we use irrigation water a lot more efficiently and grow crops in places where the climate is better suited to them. We also need to think more about nutritional water productivity: how much nutritional value are we really getting out of the water that we're putting on those crops? Should we be growing cotton here? Should we be feeding irrigated grain to livestock and getting protein and calories in a way that's so consumptive of water? There are better ways to meet our dietary needs than we're meeting them, and I really think that any chance we have of keeping the natural world

keeping the natural
world healthy and
keeping people
healthy is going to
take a pretty dramatic
change in how we
think about our
relationship to food

healthy and keeping people healthy is going to take a pretty dramatic change in how we think about our relationship to food, because of its importance in the whole water picture. **SANDRA POSTEL**

There's no doubt that population growth is impactful on conservation, and in countries where there is a small population, let's say Namibia, for example, you have a better opportunity to do conservation than in a country like Nigeria. But I'm not convinced that population itself is such a fundamental stumbling block to achieving conservation, and I would never write off a country just because it's got a lot of people in it, because often that's where the biodiversity exists.

A quirk of biogeography means that maps of biodiversity overlap with maps of population in countries like Indonesia, India, China and Mexico. These are some of the countries which have extraordinary amounts of biodiversity and extraordinary population growth rates as well. Now the challenge is going to be, how do you make conservation work in that environment? You can't just throw your hands up and say, 'No, it's gone.' You've got to do something. That's why the Nature Conservancy works in some of these countries. **M. SANJAYAN**

In the highlands of Ethiopia in particular, we're finding that agriculture is encroaching higher and higher up the mountains, and barley is now being grown at about 3500 metres [11,480 feet]. That doesn't leave much space for the remaining habitat there and the remaining wildlife, much of which is endemic to that part of the world. The populations of Simien wolves and the Walia ibex really are constrained to either the most dramatic and steep slopes in the mountains or the very highest points in the mountains, which are largely uninhabitable by people and certainly not available for agriculture, because it's too cold for most of the year. **NEVILLE ASH**

What's happened in Ethiopia and in a lot of Africa is that it's been drying out. We're all very familiar with the famines of Ethiopia, and they mainly occurred in the arid areas around the borders. What you have in the centre is a lush alpine plateau about the size of Britain – the Ethiopian highlands. It's a massive, fertile area, and as the drier areas have become uninhabitable for humans, humans have been pushed up into the mountains, into higher and higher areas, into colder environments, up to altitudes of 4000 metres [13,120 feet].

The gelada baboon is lucky in that it's the only primate in the world that lives on grass, and when you live on grass, you don't compete too much with other animals. Even as Ethiopians bring their grazing livestock into the mountains – sheep and goats – gelada baboons generally can graze alongside them. However, as farms encroach further into the Ethiopian highlands, the areas of alpine grass are shrinking, and the gelada are getting squeezed because their natural grasslands are shrinking, and the only thing left is barley crops.

We're starting to see now a much greater increase in human-gelada conflict, where the baboons are raiding barley fields because they've run out of their preferred alpine grasses. The conflict has increased dramatically, and this was never a problem ten years ago.

This is something that Ethiopia has to come to terms with on its own: how it deals with the poverty and an incredible population explosion and at the same time tries to protect some of the last remaining pockets of these very fragile mountains that are the last refuge for some of these animals.

CHADDEN HUNTER

Wetlands in general are incredibly important ecosystems. They store water and purify it, filtering out pollutants so that the water that comes out the other end is cleaner than the water that came in – and they're good at buffering floods and droughts. Wetlands worldwide have been reduced by somewhere

wetlands worldwide have been reduced by somewhere between a quarter and a half just over the past century

between a quarter and a half just over the past century. Because of the increasing demand for water, there's just so much more pressure on natural water systems. Rivers are running dry, water tables from underground aquifers are dropping, and we're seeing wetlands shrinking and declining. In just about every category of freshwater ecosystems, we're seeing serious signs that they're in ecological decline and losing health.

I think it's hard to imagine things getting better for the natural world in the next few decades, because population is continuing to increase. Our demand for water, while slowing in some areas, is continuing to increase. We've gone about meeting these human demands in a very simple way: every time we need more water, we go out and find it. We tap another river, we build another dam, we pump more groundwater. We take more out of the natural world.

in just about every category of freshwater ecosystems, we're seeing serious signs that they're in ecological decline and losing health

We're very lucky to have the natural water cycle. It is a unique and fabulous feature of the Earth. It's what gives life to this Earth, and it is something extremely precious. It's finite, though. This can be confusing.

Fresh water is renewable – we can expect rain to come every year, but only in a finite amount. There's a cycle that applies to the whole world and a cycle that applies to every watershed. There's only so much rainfall, only so much precipitation that's coming in the course of a year to that region. If we use more than the cycle is providing us, then these signs appear: the rivers run dry and groundwater tables begin to drop.

We're pumping out more water than nature is putting back in. And so it's really our interaction with the cycle – how we're using it, how we're managing it, whether we're staying within the limits of that finite supply – that determines what's happening to the natural world.

The Colorado River, in most years now, doesn't even reach the sea, and it's one of a number of important rivers in the world for which that's true – the Yellow River in China, the Nile in northern Africa, the Indus in South Asia. The Colorado is an interesting one because it rarely reaches the sea at all – not just for certain periods of the year – and this is a very clear sign that the health of the river is in pretty bad shape.

In most years the Colorado delta and the Sea of Cortez – the Gulf of California – into which the river flows, aren't getting any sustaining fresh water. There's a disconnection of eco-logical service here. The river's job is to deliver fresh water and nutrients and sediment to the delta, and it's no longer doing that work. These are important ecosystems: the delta and the upper Gulf of California are very important for fisheries; endangered species are there. But this delta has been in decline now since at least 1960, when the river stopped reaching the sea in most years after the construction of Glen Canyon Dam.

is that a productive use of water? To allow rivers to run dry in order that we might have extra green lawns in the summer time?

We have rivers running dry in fairly well watered parts of my country, the United States, in part because people are overwatering lawns in the summer time. Is that a productive use of water? To allow rivers to run dry in order that we might have extra green lawns in the summer time? I don't think so.

We have to make those choices clear, and we have to make clear what we're losing, as we keep taking more and more water out of the natural world.

SANDRA POSTEL

I can't see any scenario for our future which doesn't show wilderness shrinking and shrinking and being pushed back and back further and further into more remote enclaves – indeed, the kind of places where people probably wouldn't want to go, like completely inaccessible mountains or deserts. The bits of wilderness that are close to human settlements, that are valuable to them in one way or another, for com-mercial purposes, economic purposes, tourism, resource use, whatever it might be – those wilderness areas are incredibly endangered and will cease to be wilderness in any real sense of the term. **JONATHON PORRITT**

How many people can the Earth safely support?

Nobody knows how many people the Earth can support. The one thing we do know for sure is that human population hasn't steadily increased. It's increased in bursts, and there has never in the whole history of life on Earth been anything like what has happened over the past 50 years. In the lifetime of somebody over the age of 60 or 70, human population has trebled. And it is set by the momentum of population growth, of the children of those children who have just been born, to achieve another increase of 50 per cent or so by the middle of this century.

There are signs of it eventually slowing, and interestingly, the last couple of years mark two tipping points in human history. Fertility rates have just dropped for the first time, other than hiccups like the Black Death, below replacement levels. The other tipping point is sometime this year – next year, maybe in London, maybe in Lagos – a child is going to be born that for the first time will mark more people living in cities than in rural areas.

Three hundred years ago, only about 10 per cent of the world's population lived in cities. A century ago it was a quarter. Today it's a half. By the middle of the century, it'll be two thirds, and that makes for changes and stresses and pressures on the environment to feed the people and to get the food from where it's growing to where they are. That, we're only just beginning to wrestle with. **ROBERT MAY**

I suspect that we have more people today than we're going to have in 200 years, or perhaps even 50 years. Current projections suggest that we'll level off at somewhere between 8 billion and 9 billion, but considerable evidence indicates that we've already exceeded the long-term carrying capacity of our planet. We probably have more people than can be supported, certainly in the way that we live now.

JEFF MCNEELY

There are many examples in the biological world where species have responded to ecosystem signals, a shortage of food or other adverse changes in conditions. Our situation is different. We have the mental capacity to understand what we're doing to the planet before those limitations fully kick in, and we have the opportunity to respond before it's too late.

this survey suggested that the human total exceeded the sustainable footprint a year or so ago

JAMES LEAPE

Ecologists have a notion of carrying capacity – which is what abundance of a given population, whether it's lemmings or grasshoppers, on average over time its environment can support. And the WWF has in recent years attempted to make an estimate of what the global carrying capacity and the carrying capacity of individual countries are for people in relation to how they live. It's a necessarily imprecise calculation, but this survey suggested that the human total exceeded the sustainable footprint a year or so ago. It's a very imprecise calculation, and maybe we exceeded it longer ago, and maybe we won't exceed it for another decade or more. But it's a question that needs to be asked, and the answer ultimately depends on the assumptions you make about the lifestyle that people will have when we come to equilibrium. It is unlikely to be as lavish as that which some countries currently enjoy.

ROBERT MAY

When one tries to get at a number, my guess is somewhere between 500 million people and 1 billion. No more than that. We will see in this century the most dreadful cull, and people will be driven either to the Arctic basin, which will be the last remaining tolerable climate where food can be grown, or to smaller oases on the continents in the mountainous areas. Ironically, the origins of our species somewhere in the mountains of Kenya may be the place where people go back in Africa and are the last survivors.

People fit into the Gaia system in two ways: one, just as another animal, which we are, and we should never forget – we recycle the elements that the plants process and behave just like any other animal – but also, of course, because we're intelligent, and we've changed the whole picture of the Earth. We've started doing things that were impossible before we came along, not only in manipulating the chemistry and physics of the Earth but also in communications. In many ways, because we are part of Gaia, we are the heart and mind of the system. We've been able, through our ability, to show the Earth itself from space. It's so much more beautiful than its sister planets Mars and Venus, which of course are dead. I think we're an enormous asset to the Earth in that sense, as its heart and mind. As well as being a damaging influence, we're something special. So Gaia's going to lose just as much as us, if we don't get things right. **JAMES LOVELOCK**

Overpopulation is a significant problem, but I think the latest sets of projections coming out of the UN and other places show global population levelling off and potentially even declining at some point in the future. This is largely due to higher education levels, particularly in females, and the demographic transition. So, I think it's feasible, maybe even likely, that population pressures will begin to lessen in the future. I think our challenge is to not let natural disasters overrun that process and begin to really reduce the human population in ways that we don't want to happen, through disease and disasters. **ROBERT COSTANZA**

I think that the Earth can safely support, in a sustainable way at a reasonable standard of living, about half of what it has today. I think that would make people happier, and it would certainly make the planet happier. We'd have more diversity, we'd have plenty of productivity, we'd be able to maintain our cultural diversity, and the world would be a much more sustainable place. Choosing how to get from where we are to where we need to be is the crunch, and I have no idea how to do that. **JEFF MCNEELY**

7

Wilderness and Climate Change

Nearly everyone agrees that climate change is happening – even the sceptics only dispute the cause. So what is its effect so far on the Earth's forests, reefs, plains and polar regions and the wildlife that lives in those and other ecosystems? One point of consensus is this: among the animals on the front line are the polar bears.

In Svalbard in Spitzbergen, we were using our helicopter to try to film polar bears from the air. They're completely undisturbed by the process, and we had one extraordinary day when we were looking down on a male polar bear swimming in wonderful, broken brash ice – it was a beautiful, beautiful image and a wonderful experience. But it was absolutely clear to me how important ice coverage was for these animals. There's no doubt that people in Svalbard can see the ice breaking up. They can see the glaciers retreating. And that's a real problem for polar bears. It's going to be in the Arctic and the Antarctic that the pressure of global warming will first be obvious. **ALASTAIR FOTHERGILL**

We are rapidly losing ice cover on the North Pole. The ice cap is getting thinner, and its extent is greatly reduced. And it is that ice cap which is the home of the polar bear. So the bears are finding that the places where they're accustomed to breed and the places where they're accustomed to hunt are disappearing. Polar bears are in deep trouble, and it's most directly because of climate change. I think climate change will vary in its impacts in different habitats. It'll have a different impact on coral reefs than it does on rainforests, but across the Earth, it is likely to cause huge upheaval in ecosystems. And that's likely to be very bad for many creatures.   **JAMES LEAPE**

The Arctic is warming up by three degrees. We're told now how polar bears are drowning, and the reason they're drowning is that the icebergs and the ice cap are retreating so much that the bears suddenly find there is nowhere they can crawl out. Of course that affects their hunting of seals, and there's very, very good evidence from researchers that polar bears are having smaller litters of cubs. The cubs are smaller, and their level of nutrition is lower – that population is in severe trouble. And if, as under some projections, the whole Arctic ice cap has disappeared by 2050, then what is going to happen to the polar bear?   **MARK STANLEY PRICE**

In the 1990s, one of the big scientific challenges for us was to understand to what degree the Antarctic was vulnerable to a shift in the Earth's climate. And conventional wisdom at that stage was that the west Antarctic ice sheet was highly unlikely to melt within the next 100 to 200 years. If it did melt, it could potentially lead to an increase in sea level of tens of metres – so it would be a catastrophe. Some of the more recent evidence is suggesting that the west Antarctic ice sheet may be somewhat less stable than we thought in the mid-1990s.

ROBERT WATSON

For *Planet Earth*, I was able to go back to the Antarctic to film humpback whales bubble-netting there – extraordinary behaviour which we'd filmed about 12 years ago for the series *Life in the Freezer* – and there's absolutely no doubt that you can really see a number of changes. It's got much milder in the Antarctic peninsula. Glaciers have retreated, it's greener, and some of the penguins are changing their behaviour.

ALASTAIR FOTHERGILL

It's been very easy to see climate change in Ethiopia: as the country's been drying out, we've seen vegetation levels rising up the mountains. In about the past 30 years, we have seen the vegetation levels of the Simien Mountains climb about 30 metres [100 feet]. So in 30 years, you can look at photographs and see different tree lines moving up 30 metres.

what we're seeing in Ethiopia is humans and other animals being squeezed into these last few pockets of lush highland. So it's a problem for humans as well

What it means is that humans have been able to farm higher and higher into the mountains. It also means that the animals that survive on the alpine grasses at the very top have nowhere else to go. They've reached the top of the plateau, and so there's going to be a very interesting few decades, because we've run out of altitude. This is the jumping off point for these vegetation levels.

One problem that Ethiopia's been struggling with has been desertification. Areas where you could once farm are now arid. Areas where you could once get water have just run dry. What we're seeing in Ethiopia is humans and other animals being squeezed into these last few pockets of lush highland. So it's a problem for humans as well. They can't farm in areas where they once used to farm.

Actually one of the biggest problems in the Ethiopian highlands for humans has been erosion. Generally these people are very poor and aren't able to create terraces to hold farmland in, and a lot of the crops have only lasted, say, 10 or 20 years and then you have to move on to other parts of the mountains.

The topsoil of the Ethiopian highlands is so fragile – this thin volcanic soil – that once it gets washed away, there's absolutely no replacing it. No more volcanoes are going to lay down that topsoil, and so humans are running out of arable land in Ethiopia. They make a joke that Ethiopia's biggest export is topsoil to Egypt, because the deluge of rain each season is washing the Ethiopian topsoil down the rivers.

CHADDEN HUNTER

I'm not sure that the majority of people in this country [Kenya] understand the global concept of climate change, but they do understand what they observe locally. The Green Belt Movement holds seminars, and in every class of about 100 people, if I ask, 'How many of you know of a river that was flowing when you were a young child but is no longer flowing?', more than 60 per cent of the people will raise their hands. People understand what's happening at the very local level, but they may not understand what's happening at the polar regions or what is happening on the tops of the mountains. They do know, though, that they used to see very large chunks of glaciers on Mount Kenya and Mount Kilimanjaro, and that sometimes now, on very bright days, there is nothing to be seen.   **WANGARI MAATHAI**

How will wildernesses change as the climate changes?

Climate change is likely to be the biggest influence on the environment over the next 10 to 30 years. We've had four great ice ages over the last million and a half years. Climates have always changed, but our current climate is changing at a very rapid pace, and it's changing because we're adding greenhouse gases to the atmosphere. So how are the ecosystems going to adapt? Nobody knows for sure, but it seems safe to say that they're all going to change in different ways, but change they will.

One of the strongest influences will be the distribution of rainfall. That's important because rainfall drives the productivity of ecosystems. Greater rainfall means more productive agricultural land, for example. In areas with less rainfall, agricultural land is going to be less productive and may be used only for grazing. Historically, times of rapid climate change are times of conflict between human cultures, driven by changes in land use. They're times of great stress for ecosystems. Some will adapt and some will not. Some will adapt in ways that we cannot predict.

Consider the United Kingdom. A major factor making it liveable is the Gulf Stream. The Gulf Stream brings warm water from the equator up north almost to Greenland, and that in turn warms the air and keeps the UK liveable. With climate change, more fresh water is being pushed into the northern oceans, and that is slowing down the Gulf Stream. And it's quite possible that the Gulf Stream may even reverse, so that it will take cold water south rather than bringing warm water north. So while the world is warming, the UK may become much less liveable. You might well hope that you'll be able to grow grapes so you can have your own wine, but pretty soon you might not even be able to grow turnips.

historically, times of rapid climate change are times of conflict between human cultures, driven by changes in land use. They're times of great stress for ecosystems

On the other hand, climate change might not be bad for nature. It'll be a very bad thing for us, though, because we depend on the kind of climate that we have. We've become adapted in a very intimate way to the systems of production that we have designed and built. Climate change is going to affect us in profound and unpredictable ways. As for nature – I don't think nature cares. Nature will be able to adapt. Whether we will, as a civilization, is a very different question and perhaps a much more profound one. **JEFF MCNEELY**

Melting ice could change ocean currents. As is widely known there's a big sort of conveyor-belt system of current in the ocean, and that makes Europe habitable. As the water comes up the Atlantic and goes up between Europe and Greenland, it gets denser and eventually sinks and curves back under itself, and that's why it's called the conveyor belt. Well, historically, in geological time, it's been known to turn off, and one thing that can turn it off is a lot of melting ice water, because it'll prevent the water from becoming dense and sinking. Nobody knows a lot about that pattern, but there were reports last year which would suggest it's flickering, but we don't know whether flickering is normal or whether this is the first signal that the conveyor belt could stop abruptly, and then some of those disaster movie scenarios wouldn't seem so funny. **THOMAS LOVEJOY**

It's a matter of security if the predictions about climate change are accurate. So the melting of the icebergs and the glaciers in the world means the rise of the sea level, and some are talking about more than one metre's rise [more than three feet].

You have countries that are going to disappear – the small, island countries. You can have the best military equipment and the best technology, but what are you going to do? If your country is going to disappear, the best technology will not prevent this. So, for example, Tuvalu, a small country in the Pacific, recently requested for the country as a whole, with a 10,000 population, the status of refugee – environmental refugee – because the people are realizing that the sea is rising and their country is disappearing. **AHMED DJOGHLAF**

> some scenarios … would have Madagascar losing almost all of its remaining natural vegetation in the next 50 or 100 years

Well, there is a lot of modelling going on right now, looking at the impacts of climate change on different parts of the world. Depending on which scenarios you look at, the Amazon could be very heavily impacted, but less so, at least over the short term, than some of the areas where there's been a lot of devastation already, for instance the island of Madagascar. Some scenarios that we've been looking at would have Madagascar losing almost all of its remaining natural vegetation in the next 50 or 100 years.

The Amazon probably has a little bit more resilience than that, but if you combine the road-building that's taking place with some of the destruction that's taking place in different parts of Amazonia, and you overlay the potential for climate change, it could have drastic impacts on the Amazon. But what exactly those are going to be depends on which series of models you look at. **RUSSELL MITTERMEIER**

The issue of the oceans and climate change is, in my view, probably the most profound environmental change that I've learned about in my entire career. We have known for some time that, as the oceans have warmed in response to climate change, coral reefs, for example, have experienced more frequent bleaching events, where the coral ejects its algae partner, and we simply don't know how frequently that can happen before it's over for the coral organisms.

the issue of the oceans and climate change is, in my view, probably the most profound environmental change that I've learned about in my entire career

In addition to the warming, as the oceans absorbs CO_2 (and they absorb about one third of our emissions every year, basically saving us from having more climate change), some of that CO_2 is becoming carbonic acid, so that the oceans today are literally 30 per cent more acid than they were in preindustrial times.

As that acidity increases and it spreads deeper into the ocean, it is going to have very serious consequences for any kind of organism which builds a skeleton of calcium carbonate, whether it's a giant clam or a coral – or lots of tiny little organisms fundamental to marine ecosystems but which people don't know the names of. It's going to ripple through marine ecosystems in a very profound way.

There's no solution for it other than to deal with greenhouse gases. When we had acid rain and acid lakes, sometimes they'd add limestone to lakes, but oceans are too big for that. So it's a pretty big signal that we've just got to take on the climate-change issue.

The ocean-acidity trend is going to go through food chains. There is a constant rain of an astronomical number of tiny little organisms with calcareous shells in the upper surface waters of the ocean which live and then die and fall to the bottom. If they're there long enough, they become limestone.

That, in fact, is an important way in which the oceans regularly sequester carbon as part of their global carbon cycle, and that could stop, which would mean that you'd have more of a runaway climate-change problem.

THOMAS LOVEJOY

The fact that global warming really exists now seems to be accepted by everyone – it's just that nobody knows quite how bad it's going to become. Global warming is, of course, a major threat also to life in the seas. It will do things like change currents. It will change salinities. It's adding huge amounts of carbonic acid to the ocean. The CO_2 that is produced by burning fossil fuels becomes carbonic acid, which increases the acidity of the oceans. Now, it's all very well to worry about whales dying off, but if we create a situation in which the basic plankton on which all life depends starts to die, then that's it, that's the whole ball game. We lose everything. Everything goes. Nothing makes it.

ROGER PAYNE

Climate change is sort of a wild card for water. I think it's going to make management of water much, much more difficult. The thing that we can be pretty certain is going to happen is that the rivers that depend on mountain snow-packs for their flow are going to see that pattern of flow change significantly. More precipitation is going to fall as rain rather than snow. So the snow-pack will be less to begin with. Secondly, more of that snow-pack is going to melt earlier in the year and faster. So you're likely to get more flooding in the spring and lower flows during the drier part of the year when demands for water tend to be greater for irrigation, for hydropower, and when species tend to be stressed from low flows already. So that changing pattern of flow will impact aquatic habitats, particularly in the dry season in those river systems that depend on mountain snow-packs.

the competition for water between people and the natural world is probably going to intensify from climate change

We're talking about some of the biggest river systems in the world. All the rivers coming out of the Himalayas; all the rivers coming out of the Alps, the Andes, the Sierra Nevada the Rocky Mountains. These are big river systems and they supply millions of hectares of irrigated land, hundreds of millions of people and some very important aquatic habitats. So the competition for water between people and the natural world is going to intensify from climate change.

The thing that's important to remember about aquatic life forms is that they have, over hundreds of thousands and in some cases millions of years, become adapted to the flow pattern of the rivers in which they reside. So when something changes that's important to their habitat requirements, over the period of 20, 30, 40 years, which is a geologic twinkling of an eye, it's very hard for them to adapt quickly enough. Whether it's more flooding or more drought, it's unfamiliar. Obviously there'll be some species that adapt well and thrive, others that don't. So it will be a shift in the composition of species, and that will imply a shift in the functioning of some of those aquatic environments.

SANDRA POSTEL

On land, at the coast, where sea-level rise could be easily a metre [more than three feet] in the century – or a lot more if some other systems slip – it will be a big challenge for coastal ecosystems, and I know some conservation organizations are trying to find ways to anticipate those changes and make it easier for marshes to develop further inland as the sea-level rises.

THOMAS LOVEJOY

The climate has always changed. Why is now any different?

First of all, we're looking at climate change on a scale that hasn't happened in 650,000 years, maybe more. Second, we're looking at climate change that's happening much more quickly than ever before, which will make it much harder for ecological systems and for humans to adapt. But third, we must recognize that the Earth has been through some truly horrific climate changes in the past and ask the question why we would willingly bring such a change on ourselves.

JAMES LEAPE

The reason climate change is having a greater impact now is because both the rate of change is quicker than it has been at any other time in the last 10,000 years, but also because, coupled with climate change, we've impacted on the habitats, too. So, for example, there's a lot of fragmentation going on around the world, which reduces the ability of species to move between areas of habitat, which they might have done under past climatic changes. **NEVILLE ASH**

Well there's one real difference about the climate change that's going on at the moment, and that is that it's engineered by one species. Periods of climate change before were not engineered by biological agents – single species. And we're aware of what we're doing – at least, some of us are. So that poses a serious ethical and moral dilemma – what we're doing to other living things when we really don't have to. **THOMAS LOVEJOY**

We're in a unique time in human history right now, and this is what's really different today from 100 years in the past, 200 years in the past – we really have the capacity through technology to forecast and truly imagine the future. So if climate change had been occurring 200 years ago, I think people would have noticed it maybe even faster than we have noticed it, because they were so in tune to the rhythms of nature. But I'm not sure if they could have forecast it out into the future and said, 'OK. In the next 30 years, this is what will happen.' We can do that now. That really does give us a unique ability today to take a problem – a 100-year, a 500-year problem – and break it into manageable bite-sized chunks. **M. SANJAYAN**

Whether we like it or not, we are part of the great system Gaia. In many ways, it's helpful to think of humans as just another animal – eating plants and returning to the atmosphere the carbon dioxide that the plants need to build themselves, and also cycling nitrogen and all sorts of other elements. We are playing our part as animals. What we do as civilized humans, of course, is superimposed on that.

If that system is compromised – and it has been compromised quite a few times in the past – we know what happens. The carbon dioxide in the air builds up, and the temperature goes up with it, and it can go up as much as 8°C [14.4°F]. But there's a lot of fail-safe in the Earth's system. It's hung around an awfully long time, and it's not knocked out by something as simple as that.

Gaia will respond as it always does. It has a goal, and it has had from the beginning – to keep the planet habitable for whatever life forms happen to be in its contemporary biosphere. It will respond to what we are doing, global change, by moving to the hot state that it was in the last time – 55 million years ago – and stay there for anything up to 200,000 years, slowly sinking back to normal.   **JAMES LOVELOCK**

Over the 4-billion-year sweep of the planet's history, climate has been wildly variable. There have been times when maybe the whole planet has been a ball of snow and ice and times when exotic tropical animals have roamed the poles. But during all our recorded history, the last 6000–8000 years, the climate has been unusually steady. Earlier, when we were hunter-gatherers, we saw ice ages come and go. The steadiness of the last 6000–8000 years is thought by many to be part of the reason why we have developed civilizations. During that time, the carbon dioxide that is one of the principal greenhouse gases and blankets the Earth has remained extraordinarily steady at about 280 plus or minus 10 parts per million. Since the dawn of the industrial revolution, say around 1780, when we first started burning fossil fuels at an accelerating rate, the carbon dioxide levels have risen and the blanket has thickened.

the steadiness of the last 6000–8000 years is thought by many to be part of the reason why we have developed civilizations

> make no mistake – there is no longer any doubt that small actions now are more urgent and more important than bigger actions will be later

At first it took 150 years for us to get outside the envelope of fluctuations of the previous six to eight millennia. But by 1930 we were outside that envelope, and things really started to ramp up. There were 280 parts per million of carbon dioxide for thousands of years, up to 330 by 1960, 360 by the 1990s, 380 today. That increase of 20 parts per million in the last decade has not been seen since the end of the last ice age. The consequent effects on climate are increasingly understood but with many remaining uncertainties of detail, and it's hard to relate to it intuitively. If I tell you the temperature's changed 0.7°C [1.3°F] over the last century, and it's set to increase between 1.5°C and 6°C [2.7°F and 11°F] over the coming century, that sounds ridiculous, because the temperature changed 6°C since yesterday. But there's a huge difference between daily changes and average global temperature, year on year.

The difference in average global temperature today and the average global temperature at the depth of the last ice age is 5°C [9°F]. There are other lags that make things difficult. As the surface warms up, the oceans warm. That takes centuries. The last time the planet came to equilibrium with greenhouse gas concentrations of the kind that we're looking towards – 500 parts per million by the middle of the century – was 20 to 40 million years ago, and the oceans at that equilibrium point were about 300 feet [90 metres] higher. So it's happening slowly. Seemingly small things today commit us to consequences that will unfold over several human lifetimes. That's hard to relate to, and it's hard to gear up to act, too. But make no mistake – there is no longer any doubt that small actions now are more urgent and more important than bigger actions will be later. **ROBERT MAY**

By the middle to late 1990s, it was already clear that the Earth's climate was changing significantly. The Earth was much warmer, and precipitation patterns were already changing, and we would start to see evidence that extreme weather events were becoming more common, such as floods and droughts. Most of the world's glaciers were receding. And by the middle to late 1990s, all of the scientific evidence pointed to the fact that we humans were implicated in those changes to the Earth's climate. We couldn't validate that natural variability alone was the cause of the observed changes in climate. We have very good climatic records – surface temperature, for example – and every time we analyzed those climatic records and tried to simulate the observed changes, the observed changes could not be explained by natural phenomena such as changes in solar output or by changes in volcanic activity. The only way we could simulate those observed changes was by invoking human activities. That is to say, we were putting greenhouse gases into the atmosphere – such as carbon dioxide and methane – and it was those gases that were changing the Earth's climate.

As our knowledge improved throughout the 1990s, we started to recognize the consequences of climate change. That is to say, climate change will adversely affect most of the people on the planet; it will adversely affect agriculture in the tropics and subtropics; water resources, both the quality and the quantity; human health through an increase in the incidence of malaria, dengue fever and a water-borne disease, cholera; and biodiversity and ecological systems, especially systems such as coral reefs.

Each one of the Intergovernmental Panel on Climate Change reports, from 1991 to 2001, placed the message firmly in front of the policymakers that the Earth's climate was changing primarily due to human activities and that most of the impacts would be negative. A key question is whether this had an impact on policymakers. Policymakers negotiated and then signed the United Nations framework on climate change in 1992.

by the middle to late 1990s, all of the scientific evidence pointed to the fact that we humans were implicated in those changes to the Earth's climate many of the governments of the world are listening and starting to take action. Many in the private sector are listening and starting to take action

And then they negotiated the Kyoto Protocol in 1997. It has been ratified by enough countries that it has now entered into force and is now being implemented. Unfortunately, not all OECD countries have ratified it, including the US and Australia. I do believe to a large measure that people are listening. Many of the governments of the world are listening and starting to take action. Many in the private sector are listening and starting to take action. But we have a long, long way to go to truly protect the Earth's climate.

ROBERT WATSON

One of the really interesting and quite spooky things is that basically all recorded history of our species, and a lot of prehistory, occurred in this 10,000-year period of relative climate stability – which basically means that the human enterprise is based on the notion that the climate won't change.

Of course we know from the history of climate on Earth that it will change sooner or later. When climate change takes place, even if it's natural climate change, it's going to be rough for civilization, and it will be rough for life on Earth, because in this instance it will be climate change, together with a highly modified landscape, which makes it much harder for species to disperse and follow their required conditions. If cities or agricultural land are in the way, it will be much harder for species to move.

One thing we know from geological history is that in times of climate change ecosystems do not just sort of pick up and move as biological communities. Each individual species moves in its own direction and its own way. So basically you have ecosystems disassembling and completely novel ones assembling in locations that are rather hard to predict. So the only solution for that kind of response to climate change is to make it easier for species to move.

THOMAS LOVEJOY

In recent times, in the last ten years, but in the last two years in particular, the science on climate change has become ever more alarming and ever more urgent in its message of the need for solutions to be implemented.

the first thing we need is an intergovernmental treaty that's going to set the right kind of targets and frameworks for nations to take action

And to that extent, we've now put this campaign at the heart of what we're doing both in this country and at the global level through Friends of the Earth International, campaigning for both intergovernmental agreements and for national action to meet the challenge.

We don't have a lot of time. There is really a sense that if we don't do something within the next 15 years, then it might be too late. So we do have to prioritize action on carbon dioxide emissions and the other greenhouse gases and to limit the concentrations of those substances in the atmosphere to an acceptable level before it's too late.

That is a very challenging agenda, because the world presently is run on fossil fuels, and the increasing demand for fossil fuels in some developing countries, in Asia in particular, is going to make it extremely difficult to get across the solutions in time, whether that be through technologies or changes in consumption patterns. We probably need both. But in any event, we need an intergovernmental treaty that's going to set the right kind of targets and frameworks for nations to take action. And at the moment we're lacking that.   **TONY JUNIPER**

How can there still be sceptics? And what do they say?

I think that when you're talking about global warming, you have to examine what we know conclusively. And that is that the Earth's temperature, after going through a cooling period, has risen by 1°C over the past century. At the same time carbon dioxide emissions have risen 30 per cent.

What is still uncertain is what impact, if any, man is having on this warming. There was a study reported just last week, a study of core samples taken from beneath the Arctic Ocean. And these core samples, which are the best timeline of the Earth's history, according to scientists, show that the North Pole was actually a subtropical climate that was around 75 degrees I think 55 million years ago. What is the reason for that? Clearly it wasn't man, it wasn't cars, it wasn't factories.

There are so many variables that go into climate science, that to make a blanket statement or try to pinpoint just one variable as being the be-all and end-all is really shortsighted.   **PEYTON KNIGHT**

I don't know how people can doubt the reality of climate change. The issue, of course, is not whether or not the climate is changing, because it very clearly is, but the extent to which we are responsible and the extent to which a change in our behaviour could ameliorate that change in the climate.

It was perfectly responsible for people 20 years ago to say, 'Look, we don't have the evidence. We don't have the continuity of statistics needed to tell us enough about the rate at which we're changing, to say whether or not human beings are responsible.'

Over that 20 years, however, the evidence has accumulated until now, it seems to me, absolutely incontrovertible. Ninety per cent of scientists who are in any way concerned with this will say that humanity has contributed to the change.

Those are the issues, not just whether in fact there's climate change. There *is* climate change.

DAVID ATTENBOROUGH

I do think it's good to be sceptical about man's impact on global warming, just considering what man seems to be learning on a daily basis. Thirty years ago we were talking about the little ice age that was coming, and now it's warming, and I think there's a lot of misinformation out there.

When talking about global warming, it is important to differentiate the exaggerations from the facts. What we've seen, what we know, what the models predict and what is going into those models, in a lot of instances, can be garbage in, garbage out. Some of the most prominent global-warming alarmists out there, including scientists in the United States, have been off by orders of magnitude on their past predictions. That would indicate that we have a lot more studying to do, especially before we start taking ill-fated precautions such as the Kyoto Protocol.

There are plenty of scientists out there who aren't being heard from because the media tend to like a sensational story like global warming. Richard Lindzen of the Massachusetts Institute for Technology and Research has noted time and again how funding seems to find its way only to scientists who are willing to promote certain scientific models and studies that promote the idea that man is causing the climate to become catastrophically warmer.

So it's a follow-the-money issue, and I know that there are a lot of scientists out there who simply aren't being heard from, based on who the media choose to cover. **PEYTON KNIGHT**

I truly believe that Americans living in the heartland of this country can accept and understand the notion that they may have to change their lifestyles in order to make the entire world a better place. The Nature Conservancy sent me to southern Arizona some months ago, and I was in a room full of ranchers. These are guys wearing cowboy hats, and they've got their cattle dogs, and they've got their Carhartt jackets on. I watched them listen to a talk on climate change. The guy up there was saying to them, 'Do you know last year was the first year in southern Arizona that there was no frost on the ground?' And every cattleman in that room nodded his head. And I thought to myself, you know what?

These guys get climate change. They get climate change better than any politician out here, because if there's no frost on the ground, it means they're going to have a hell of a fire season, and it's going to have a major impact on how they're going to be able to graze their cattle that year.

So I think these environmental issues are finally coming down to sort of roost in the heartland of America, and I think that's where you're going to see some change.   **M. SANJAYAN**

man-made global warming is very much in question and certainly there is no solution that can be taken that would not, in terms of reducing carbon dioxide, have a dramatic negative impact on the economic output

I would say that the science is most uncertain. There are a lot of scientists, including over 17,000 who have signed the Oregon Institute of Science and Medicine petition that, in effect, says 'Man-made global warming is very much in question,' and certainly there is no solution that can be taken that would not, in terms of reducing carbon dioxide, have a dramatic negative impact on the economic output of first-world nations and the development of third-world nations. It would create even more environmental problems, keep many of the environmental problems that exist in third-world nations in place. That's the problem. It's very short sighted to only look at one environmental problem and ignore all the others that could possibly be created by taking steps to cure it, especially when that environmental problem is really very much in question right now.   **PEYTON KNIGHT**

It's important to recognize that there is astounding consensus in the scientific community on this issue: that climate change is happening and that human emissions of carbon into the atmosphere is the principal cause. So it's time to ignore the sceptics. There will always be doubters of anything, any phenomenon like this. And let's not forget, there are powerful economic forces at work – industries that are concerned that action on climate change may be to their disadvantage. So in the end it's not that surprising that some voice doubts.   **JAMES LEAPE**

it's important to recognize that there is astounding consensus in the scientific community on this issue: that climate change is happening and that human emissions of carbon into the atmosphere is the principal cause

Achieving scientific understanding is a complex process, and in the early stages of an ill-understood phenomenon, lots of ideas contend. When you come across a new phenomenon – whether it's HIV when it first appeared or the suggestion that smoking causes lung cancer or the idea that burning fossil fuel is going to thicken the greenhouse gas blanket and cause climate change – there will be huge uncertainties and lots of different opinion. As time goes on, you gather information, you do experiments, ideas coalesce, and you arrive at an understanding.

If you take the case of HIV, for quite a while in the late 1980s, even after it had become crystal clear that the virus HIV is the organism that causes Aids, there were people who felt that maybe other factors had to be implicated. By now, that HIV causes Aids is a fact as sure as Newton's inverse square law of gravitation, but I could still assemble a travelling roadshow of people, including one Nobel Laureate, who would tell you HIV doesn't cause Aids. Still some people believe smoking doesn't cause lung cancer, and certainly people say passive smoking is no harm at all.

The motives are sometimes a stubborn human desire to cling to a theory that has been shown to be false, and sometimes it has more venal associations, as in the case of the tobacco lobby.

In the case of the climate-change denials, you have all of those kinds of factors. You have people who are genuinely clinging to sceptical

there's also, to the
tune of tens of
millions of dollars, and
quite demonstrably,
a hydrocarbon-based
lobby, which has very
direct analogues with
the tobacco lobby

positions or people who are just emphasizing the remaining uncertainties that do exist. But there's also, to the tunes of tens of millions of dollars, and quite demonstrably, a hydrocarbon-based lobby, which has very direct analogues with the tobacco lobby.

The science academies of the G8, plus China, Brazil and India, are all signed up to a thing that says climate change is real, important, serious and we've got to do something about it. There will still be people, some for honest but muddled scientific reasons, stubbornly clinging to an indefensible view, and others for more self-interested venal motives, as perhaps certain segments of the hydrocarbon lobby.   **ROBERT MAY**

A lot of the people who are campaigning against action on climate change – because they say it's not true or it's not to do with people, and even if it is to do with people, then we shouldn't worry about it because it's going to do so much damage to the economy that we should let the pollution just carry on emitting from power stations and vehicles – the people who say that mostly aren't coming from a scientific perspective.

They're working in a political context, and what they're trying to do very often is to protect a particular industry, whether that's the motor industry, the oil industry or the coal industry.

Happily, those people have become fewer in number in recent years. There are a few diehards out there but their voice is becoming much more marginal. Even in the US now, those people are getting little airtime, and even when they are getting airtime, they're getting criticisms back even from some of the mainstream media organizations that previously were quite sympathetic to them.   **TONY JUNIPER**

Where Has Environmentalism Gone Wrong?

The modern environment movement is about 40 years old. Throughout we have heard passionate pleas to save whales, tigers, the oceans – all sorts of species and ecosystems and even the planet itself. Yet sometimes things seem to be as bad as ever. Have the non-governmental organizations and conservation movement been getting it wrong? Have environmentalists failed to learn from the past? Or, on the other hand, would the world be a whole lot worse off if there had never been an environmental movement?

I'm not sure the conservation organizations have got it wrong in terms of where their focus has been. It's just that their focus has been at one end of the spectrum. You know, we – conservation biology and the conservation movement – were formed as a crisis discipline. We were formed in the sixties and the seventies by influential fathers and mothers of the movement who talked about things like the population explosion and the extinction vortex and *Silent Spring* – words that incited us to sit up and go, 'My God. Things are going to get really bad really quickly.' And people went out there and tried to do conservation based on this fear of the world collapsing – literally, the world collapsing.

Just think about the times, the sixties and seventies, and the kinds of revolutions, social revolutions that were going on at that time. What happened is, I think, the conservation movement just stopped evolving ultimately, if our movement is not relevant to the lives of real people dealing with real issues, then we're just going to be preaching to the choir

after that. You know, we got it right in starting the movement, but we didn't keep up with the times. So when we do campaigns that say 'Save the Tiger' or 'Save the Whale' and focus on a species, that's clearly important, but the conservation movement has to go well, well beyond that. Ultimately, if our movement is not relevant to the lives of real people dealing with real issues, then we're just going to be preaching to the choir. **M. SANJAYAN**

The environment movement has had some enormous successes over the last three decades or so. For example, river-water quality in some western countries now is much better. We've managed to do a lot about things such as acid rain and other air-pollution challenges, the damage to the ozone layer and phasing out the chemicals that were causing that problem. But at the same time, the challenges have in some ways got bigger. Our consumption of natural resources, the pressure on land and the changes now taking place with the climate pose far bigger challenges than those that have been solved.

We have to look at ways in which we can start gearing up the environmental message to be something more than simply an add-on to the way we do development and run our countries. We need to make it something that's at the centre of the way in which governments and societies work, and we're still far from doing that. **TONY JUNIPER**

Forgive us, we knew not what we did. We were unaware of the consequences of all kinds of things that we were doing. The whole notion of greenhouse gases was unperceived 50 years ago. It never occurred to anybody that we could be changing the climate, just as it never occurred to anyone that we could actually poison the oceans, because the oceans were infinitely large. Well, both those things were wrong.

So, yes, our opinions have changed, and so they should as we become wiser, as we understand the evidence more clearly. Of course, the situation is, in fact, worse than it was. That's because there are very many more people living on Earth, and so the problems have become even greater. Had the non-governmental organizations not been doing things, it would have been very, very much worse than it is now. So I don't have any doubt about the value of the work of the NGOs.

There will always be a question as to whether this or that particular policy is the correct one – whether we're achieving the right balance in educating people to understand what's happening in the world around them – whether we should be putting fences round reserves and so on. Those are the problems of detail. But that there should be elements within society which are concerned about doing what they can, about examining the problems and working to solve them – of course there should be. And of course there've been mistakes. Of course. We're human beings. But I'm absolutely persuaded that the world would be in a far worse situation had it not been for the non-governmental organizations that have taken on the conservation issues.

> had the non-governmental organizations not been doing things, it would have been very, very much worse than it is now

DAVID ATTENBOROUGH

I don't think the environmental movement has got it wrong. I think the problems would be a great deal worse if the environmental movement hadn't got it right up until now. And people sometimes forget that the progress that we've seen on new legislation, on improved air and water quality, on biodiversity, on all of these things – although it's not good enough – wouldn't have happened without the environmental movement.

So it's not that environmentalists got it wrong; it's just that they haven't been as successful as they should have been or could have been.

JONATHON PORRITT

where has environmentalism gone wrong?

I'm not sure that the environment movement or the conservation movement has really got things wrong. What it has been fighting against are forces which are so powerful, so influential at government level, that I doubt that really anything better could have been done. Where perhaps they – all of us – have failed, is to find a point of engagement with the natural world. When I say the natural world, I mean the whole living structure in which we're embedded and which we're talking about.

RICHARD MABEY

we haven't historically paid enough attention to the fundamental drivers of the destruction of nature – the fundamental economic forces that are really causing the destruction

If you look back over the last 30 or 40 years of conservation and look at the challenges of today, you would reach several conclusions. One is that, 40 years ago, even sometimes only 10 years ago, we simply were not acting on a large-enough scale. We were doing too much at a local level, and that didn't add up to the kind of global impacts that are necessary if we're really going to turn the corner, if we're really going to get the planet onto a sustainable path.

So we need to find ways to have an impact on a scale that matters globally. We haven't historically paid enough attention to the fundamental drivers of the destruction of nature – the fundamental economic forces that are really causing the destruction in forests and coral reefs all over the world. How do we get at those? How do we begin to change markets so that markets provide incentives for conservation, so that markets are harnessed for conservation and aren't driving destruction? Those are the kinds of strategies that I think hold the most promise for the future.

JAMES LEAPE

The global conservation movement has made mistakes and has corrected them as it has gone along. I've been on the board of directors of most of the major conservation organizations during the past 25 years, and I've seen how we evolved, the mistakes we made, how we corrected them and so on. And among those mistakes was, early on, concentrating on just a few charismatic species. We ignored places where there weren't tigers or pandas and so on, and we therefore allowed a lot of very valuable environment to shrink still more.

The second mistake was that of omission, to not pay enough attention to the needs of the people where the reserves have to be set up. You can't put a fence around the reserve and a sign on it and then go away or leave a guard or two. You've got to involve the people, and you have to make it worth their while in terms of jobs, new income and so on. But a lot of progress has been made. Every case is different, but we know how to do it now. We know how to approach a country or an area where a reserve needs to be set up, although it takes money and it takes a lot of effort to do that.

Another mistake, I guess, is in the image of these environmentalists swarming down from the countries of the north and telling people how to run their affairs. And there's the north-south rift that developed where most of the developing countries were saying to the north, 'OK, you've got the money, we've got the biodiversity. What are you putting on the table? Why are you coming and telling us what to do, and you're not contributing anything?' Well I guess that's a very good objection, and we now know that we have to handle that carefully right from the get-go.

I think it's been solved in part by the programmes set in motion everywhere to increase economy as environmental protection is increased. But it's such a huge problem worldwide that we just haven't got the resources now to make it happen. We've got to get the world aware of what this means to their future, their long-term future, and to get a global conservation movement that becomes routine, as part of political agendas, supported by people who in the same way they insist on having an army and insist on having jobs, they need to insist that their environment is preserved

insist on it happening. In the same way they insist on having an army and insist on having jobs, they need to insist that their environment is preserved. And when we get to that point – and I think it's likely to be a tipping point, where it becomes suddenly the thing, the big thing to know about – then you'll get a lot of progress. **E.O. WILSON**

Have the developed countries imposed their views on the developing world?

I think that too many promoters of environmental restrictions for the Third World are actually under the misguided notion that, if everybody developed like the First World, we would have even more problems. That's why they promote irrational uses like solar and wind, where the technology doesn't exist to viably provide for the energy needs of any developing country. That's the main problem: people from the First World trying to impose their environmental will on the Third World, to the detriment of Third World indigenous peoples. **PEYTON KNIGHT**

> if I look at the big American organizations, they've got a world view shaped by American values, American practice, American dollars. And they are out there imposing that view wherever they can

Over the years, if I look at the big environmental conservation organizations, they've certainly recognized the importance of local and cultural sensitivity, differentiated approaches to different problems in different countries. However, the truth is that there are still some very big macho approaches to conservation out there.

If I look at the big American organizations, they've got a world view shaped by American values, American practice, American dollars. And they're out there imposing that view wherever they can, in order to accelerate their particular conservation mission.

Have they learnt the lessons of the last 30 years about some of the necessary patterns of partnership and a more sensitized approach to working with other countries and other peoples? I'm not sure, in all honesty.

I still don't really see enough humility in the behaviour and the positioning of big environmental organizations. I still see a rather dehumanized approach to conservation that still puts human beings second in the heap of priorities in order to pursue the business of putting nature and animals first. And because I'm a sustainable-development activist, not an environmental activist as such, that still causes me considerable pain, because I know it won't work in the long run.

JONATHON PORRITT

I read in a newspaper report only two weeks ago that China was buying up a huge tract of land in Borneo so they could have the hardwood they needed, not only for the upcoming Olympics, but in general, for the construction industry. Some local indigenous people were interviewed, and the elder basically said, 'I've been trying to protect my forest for decades. However, the younger people now want roads. They want education. They want a lifestyle that is more consistent with a Western lifestyle. Therefore, we have made a decision that we are willing to sacrifice our indigenous lifestyle for things such as televisions and other capitalistic goods.'

And it's very easy for me, living in Washington DC, and having lived in London, with all of the trappings of a Western society, a capitalistic society, to say to people in a developing country, 'You shouldn't make the same mistakes we made.' And therefore I believe each individual country, and each individual community must make its own decisions. The key issue is that people need to be informed of what the consequences of

so often we say we'll protect an area, and then we cut all the way around it, and in the end, even that protected area suffers through erosion and changes in the ecosystem

their decisions are. They need to know that this is what they have today and what they would have tomorrow.

I believe we need to protect some nature – there's no question in my mind about it. In fact, protect a lot of nature, basically. But is it up to us in the West to tell local indigenous people what they should or shouldn't do with their land? It's a real dilemma.

I would love the OECD countries to lead by example. Unfortunately, even in some OECD countries, we're still converting some of our natural forests. In the western United States, we are still logging 1000-year-old redwood forests. I find this totally unacceptable, and I think it's almost a crime to cut down these redwood trees that are hundreds, if not thousands, of years old. I would argue that a country as rich as the United States should be able to protect those remnant forests, and that there must be some other way to get the type of wood we need for construction and other uses.

Personally, I would protect these very old-growth forests, and I would make sure that not only is the forest protected, but also the boundary around the forest is protected. So often we say we'll protect an area, and then we cut all the way around it, and in the end, even that protected area suffers through erosion and changes in the ecosystem.

ROBERT WATSON

I think it's really important that we don't take the moral high ground in talking about conservation or the environment. I honestly don't think any country can afford to take the moral high ground. No-one's done it right. But there are individuals within all these countries, whether it's in Sri Lanka or in Kenya or in the United States, who see a different path, see a better way.

When you go and talk to a bunch of school kids in Kenya about the environment and you come at it with an open mind and with humility, people are willing to give you the benefit of the doubt. They understand inconsistencies between individuals and government. They understand the inconsistencies between what one might desire and what one can achieve. And when you have someone just say, 'Well, you have no business coming here and telling us what we're doing because you're screwing up your own country,' in general I think they're just reacting. These are people who are going to react to that because they have some other agenda. Honest, well-meaning, thoughtful people, in the dialogues that I have had working for the Nature Conservancy, have rarely brought that as an argument to me.   **M. SANJAYAN**

> there are individuals within all these countries, whether it's in Sri Lanka or in Kenya or in the United States, who see a different path, see a better way

I think the environmental movements, until very recently, were absolutely obsessed with the interests of northern countries and disrespectful of poor people and the whole dynamic of their societies. So I think the first UN Conference on the Environment in Rio was very northern dominated and had the idea that development has got to stop and we've got to conserve more.

In Tanzania, they established big animal parks that rich tourists came to, and the country encouraged this because it brought in tourist dollars. The people who used to live on those lands lived in villages at the side, and they used to go and hunt and poach and kill the animals. And they were quite angry about it all, because in the aim of conserving nature, they'd lost their lands and lost their livelihoods. We started to change, to say they should have control over managing the animal parks. So they controlled licences for hunting. Then they had the money, and then they built a school for their children. They all started sleeping under malaria nets and not getting malaria. So I think the early environmental movement – that's

it's bringing a kind of revolutionary set of question-marks that look at development in a new way.
I don't think the transformation has taken place, but I think they're on the edges of it

just one example – was very disrespectful of the poor and their need for development and very much imposed a northern view on the world that just can't work.

If I skip on to the trade talks in Seattle, the NGOs and a lot of the northern countries were saying, 'We're going to impose rules on international trade that say, if you don't respect the environment, you can't engage in international trade.' And all the poor countries were saying 'How dare you? We're not able to fulfil your environmental conditions, and now you're going to squeeze us out of the world economy. Having used us and polluted the world, and you've taken all the riches, and we've got very little, now you're going to make rules that mean we won't be able to grow our economies or export what we have.'

We saw then that we weren't going to get any international environmental agreements at all if it was us telling the poor world what they had to do. And I think it took the environmental movement a long time to embrace the right to development for the poor – because it had become anti-development because development had led to the destruction of forests and even more strain on the resources of the world.

There's been a lot of changed thinking in the World Bank. I think the early assumptions about development were, let's have lots of projects, lots of roads, lots of dams. Infrastructure means development, it means civilization. People were moved. All sorts of habitats were destroyed. People's livelihoods were destroyed. I think a lot of that was enormously crass and destructive, and countries ended up with the capacity to produce electricity they weren't using. There have been terrible errors.

I think the assumption about development, until very recently, has been that our kind of society is developed and is civilized, and everyone else is going to have what we have. And I think it's just now dawning that that's undoable and not attractive. I now think it's bringing a kind of revolutionary set of question-marks that look at development in a new way. I don't think the transformation has taken place, but I think they're on the edges of it.

CLARE SHORT

In the past, the World Bank focused on big infrastructure projects: roads, dams, and power plants. And the evidence now suggests that many of those older projects were not as successful as we would have liked. They did not actually alleviate poverty and help the rural poor, and in particular, some of the road projects went through major pristine forest areas. As we put a road through a pristine forest area, we ended up with degradation and loss of these natural ecological systems. The World Bank made a major breakthrough in the early 1990s when it started to develop the so-called safeguard policies: protecting natural habitats, making sure the environment is not adversely affected, looking after the rights of indigenous people and making sure there wasn't involuntary settlement without appropriate compensation.

The World Bank has ten safeguard policies, and we apply them in every development project, but we do have to recognize there are trade-offs. Not everything is a win-win situation. Therefore we look very carefully at what will truly alleviate poverty or stimulate sustainable economic growth. But as we do that analysis, we try to identify any adverse implications, either on local people or on the environment, including natural habitats. In the past, many of our infrastructure projects did lead to the loss of biodiversity without even helping the local rural poor, but we are now designing our projects in a much more holistic manner.

The World Bank is now doing much more work with local communities, in

in the past, many of our infrastructure projects did lead to the loss of biodiversity without even helping the local rural poor, but we are now designing our projects in a much more holistic manner

order to understand their desires and aspirations. It is called community-driven development. What we've recognized is that if we have top-down design of a park or some agricultural project, it's likely to fail if we don't work with and involve local communities. More and more, the Bank has recognized there has to be ownership at the local community level in both the design and the implementation of the projects. If local people are involved in the design and implementation, the project is far more likely to be successful. We are trying to understand local culture far more, local value systems far more, and this is moving us, at least now, in the right direction.

Some further loss of rainforests is absolutely inevitable, as well as some further loss of mangrove and other grassland systems, just because of the expanding populations in those areas. However, I do believe we can form far better partnerships between developed and developing countries, and the onus is on us, the developed countries, to help provide financial support to those countries, so they don't have to destroy their ecosystems. Their ecosystems have value at both the local and global level, and we have to work in partnership, providing better technologies and some financial assistance, so the rate of tropical deforestation can be reduced. **ROBERT WATSON**

Was the formation of national parks and exclusive zones for wildlife a good thing?

Well, I think conservation initially was the system of creating a series of islands of safety, and you didn't have to worry about what happened outside. But what people are realizing more and more is there is no inside or outside. The boundaries that people were trying to create are not protected by fences – they are permeable. People can come in, and we think of them as poachers, but the animals go out, and the animals cause a considerable

> what people are realizing ... is there is no inside or outside. The boundaries ... are permeable

amount of harm to the people that live in those general areas. I think fortress conservation is being increasingly abandoned everywhere. There's a recognition that the space that was set aside, either as a refuge or as something meant to be self-sustaining, is simply too small. Animals need huge areas. The climate varies. Some places were founded at the base of Mount Kilimanjaro – the streams are changing. Everything moves. And so if you try to keep things safely fenced, you're going to trap animals in an area that may not be the best place for them in the future.

CRAIG PACKER

To conserve a habitat, we say, 'We're going to protect this area by law, and we'll save it by prohibiting every negative human influence.' But then we must exclude people who had prior claims to the resources, replace them with tourists who may bring in exotic species of weeds or diseases, stop air pollution and climate change and create artificial boundaries where none existed before. Is this really the best we can do?

What about a slightly different scenario, where people have a sustainable relationship with the land, where different parts of the landscape are allocated for different uses? Part of the area may be sufficiently large to support enough wildlife to conserve tigers or is connected to other areas which together are large enough, and this part of the landscape is managed with that objective, with compatible human uses. Another area is much smaller, but contains wild relatives of domesticated plants, and we manage that area to conserve those species. Another area is allocated to extensive agriculture that can have some interaction with the protected areas, depending on them for clean water.

Interaction between the different land-uses, rather than fences, would be better for managing our landscape. And it may be that these

what about a slightly different scenario, where people have a sustainable relationship with the land, where different parts of the landscape are allocated for different uses?

different landscapes will give us a greater capacity to adapt to change than land-use that is static, like a fortress. Very few of history's fortresses lasted very long; they were easy targets. A scenario of adapting to change through having a range of land-uses and a range of ways of managing resources is a much more viable adaptation and likely to be more successful in conserving biodiversity.

What we're trying to conserve is the capacity of an ecosystem to adapt to changing conditions, because we know that the conditions will change. How do we maintain the capacity to adapt to change? We maintain species richness to the maximum extent, enabling species interactions. We avoid pollution, avoid external disruptions like invasive species and enable the traditional human uses that formed the current landscape. To me, this is a recipe for successful protected areas.

One of our challenges is that establishing protected areas requires us to put boundaries around them. This land is protected – here's the boundary defined by law. The people living outside the boundary own their land, so they behave in certain ways. They are permitted to enter the protected sanctuary only under certain conditions and denied benefits that long were theirs. That approach doesn't work very well in an ecological sense because the ecosystems are the way they are at least partly because of past human influences and, in any case, will move with changing climates. One of our big challenges in the coming years is how to manage these ecosystems that we've legally established as protected areas, for reasons that are important to us culturally, and enable them to adapt to the changing climatic and economic conditions, which might require their boundaries to move.

In some parts of the world, a fortress mentality may be necessary for a moment in history. But it's not necessarily a long moment; it's at a time of particular stress. After a few years, perhaps a decade or two at the most, we can start to soften the boundaries. We can start to recognize that a protected area should be surrounded by forests that are managed for other reasons – for sequestering carbon or producing timber, or for using the land in ways that are compatible with the protected-area objectives.

JEFF MCNEELY

Creation of protected areas is often referred to as a kind of fortress mentality. I think that's a distraction. National parks with hard boundaries have a future. They are in many different places a cornerstone for conservation, or an essential part of a broader conservation strategy. But these parks will not be enough by themselves. We risk turning them into islands of green in a sea of destruction if we're not careful, and that won't work for protecting the long-term ecosystem values that are important to us.

> one has to pay attention to what's happening outside those protected areas, in the broader landscape

One needs to recognize that the safeguarding of some habitats through protected area is an essential piece of an overall conservation strategy. It's also not enough by itself. One has to pay attention to what's happening outside those protected areas, in the broader landscape upon which many species depend and on which the health of the ecosystem depends. In many cases, some continued human use may well also be possible. It depends of course on the nature of the ecosystem and on the nature of the use. But clearly, in any system, one needs to find a path where conservation can coexist with developments necessary to meet the needs and aspirations of the people who live there. That must be a standard in any conservation effort.

JAMES LEAPE

Currently the slogan is that the locals are involved, but it's not true. It's the bigwigs, it's the politicians or it's the NGOs. It's not the average person who lives with the snow leopard. It's not the local in that village. They

currently the slogan is that the locals are involved, but it's not true. It's the bigwigs, it's the politicians or it's the NGOs

are still hand-to-mouth. In fact, whenever national parks are created, some of the people are pushed out of their livelihoods and their established habitat. The thing to do right away is to compensate them, educate them and draw them into these NGOs and local organizations. Draw them into these government departments rather than alienating them. That is the biggest problem. You have the money, you have the resources but you're alienating the people who are key – the locals on the ground. To me, it's as simple as that. **NISAR MALIK**

I think it's very sad that people are talking more and more about a very tight set of specially protected conservation areas, refuges if you like, in the midst of the human-dominated world. I don't think that'll last. You can keep humans out for a given length of time, but ultimately they will encroach and take over. It's a sign of desperation, to be honest, that that approach to fortress conservation is becoming more and more favoured in the environment movement. But we have to find a better accommodation between humankind and the natural world than is offered down that particular route.

I think at the heart of what conservation offers people for the future is a balance between human intervention in the natural world and leaving enough space for those natural systems to carry on providing us with the functions, the value, the service – all those benefits that we derive from the natural world.

Of course we need to keep some special wilderness places special. That will always be the case. But I don't really think that, when you're talking about very heavily populated countries, you're going to find that many spaces that fit into that category in the future.

However, I think it's clear now that if we really want to maintain some species, then even very tightly controlled, well-managed tourism, access, recreation – whatever it might be – isn't going to be possible.

And I'm thinking of some of the great apes, of the situation in Botswana in the Okavango delta. I'm thinking of some of the wilderness areas in Canada and America. It's only if you can keep the level of intervention, of access, so low that it almost makes no difference, that you might still be able to think about some accommodation. But the tourism volume now is so huge, that I just don't see how we'll be able to handle that. And I suspect that more and more countries will move towards some completely protected sites as the proper companion piece, if you like, to managed wildlife conservation and tourism in other areas.

if we really want to maintain some species, then even very tightly controlled, well-managed tourism, access, recreation – whatever it might be – isn't going to be possible

JONATHON PORRITT

I think one of the biggest problems we have with protecting these last pockets of pristine environment now is deciding who has the right to go in there.

We have indigenous people who might have used that land and those animals as a resource for generations. We have conservationists, biologists, people who want to protect them. A lot of us want to protect them, but the question is, who has the right to access them? If we lock them up, who are we locking them up for?

In a case like the Simien Mountains, we have 6000 people living inside the national park. We have ecotourists coming in who would probably prefer to see the mud huts removed from the cliff edge, but it really raises that question: who are these animals for? Who is this environment for? And we'll have a situation where we have well protected environmental areas so locked up that only an elite few can go in and visit these animals. In 50 years time, an Ethiopian probably will not be able to afford to see a Walia ibex, an iconic animal from their own country, and yet we're setting up tourism to lock up these few gems.

CHADDEN HUNTER

Does the environmental movement really address the main issues?

I think one of the huge underlying problems with conservation at the moment is the way that we're not addressing poverty. I think that this concept of conserving specific animals, say a rare mammal which is very charismatic, is something that appeals to the West. It appeals to scientists who fall in love with the charisma of these animals. And yet I really worry about the progress we'll make as conservationists unless we start to deal with the poverty in these countries.

I really worry about the progress we'll make as conservationists unless we start to deal with the poverty in these countries

You just can't go to somebody who's trying to feed their children and talk about the conservation of a wolf or a whale. It just doesn't mean anything. And so we can deal with some of the symptoms and try and stick some band-aids on these last few pockets of environment, but it really is not going to be addressing the core problem: the poverty that surrounds a lot of these environments.   **CHADDEN HUNTER**

I think that there's an incredible disconnect now between the forces in the developed nations and the realities on the ground. People who claim to love animals so much are the ones that see, in the safety of their homes, beautiful pictures in beautiful light of a female lion playing with her cubs. They have no idea what that lion can do to people that have to live next to it. They have no idea that these animals actually cause serious damage to people.

We're seeing 100 people a year in Tanzania attacked by lions. Three quarters of those are killed. We're seeing thousands of people who are losing their livestock, thousands of people who are losing their crops to elephants. This is very serious. These are people who are on the edge of existence. The loss of their crop may seem like just a few pounds of maize to us, but to them that's their livelihood. How are they going to survive and support their families for the next year?

So what do you expect them to do? Are you just going to wave your finger at them and say, 'Be nice to the nice big elephant?' 'Oh that – sorry about the lion. That's really cute, though. Look at the baby – isn't that sweet?' They're not going to listen to that. Why should they care? They think we're crazy.

We had a project recently where we were trying to figure out how lions actually survive in one of the man-eating areas. It was very hard to get a radio collar on it. We spent a month trying to do this. In the end we captured a leopard. But we weren't interested in the leopard, and so after we'd caught the leopard we let it go. And all the local people were shocked. They said, 'Why did you let it go? Why didn't you kill it?' You can read in the newspapers out here almost every week of a story where a lion has been captured that was either killing people or killing cattle. You quote the people in the newspapers. What they say when they've killed the lion – they're so pleased – are things like, 'You know, to us that lion was worth less than the skin of an old goat.' It has no value to them whatsoever. It's a pain. It's a pest.

CRAIG PACKER

what they say when they've killed the lion ... are things like, 'You know, to us that lion was worth less than the skin of an old goat.' It has no value to them whatsoever. It's a pain. It's a pest

The NGOs come in with concepts, with ideas that they are trying to implement. The reality on the ground is very different. First of all, they're training up locals who do not have the education. So the park rangers, who have not even a fifth-grade degree, are told in a few power point slides that this is what the footprint of a snow leopard is like or this is what the animal is like and this is what we want. Now, when these people go out, there are times – we've seen it ourselves – where we've been shown wolf tracks or we've been shown totally different kills with various bite marks on them which couldn't be a snow leopard – it doesn't kill that way, or it doesn't leave those prints. The problem is there is so little scientific research. Anyone coming from the West first of all has to understand the culture, the system, the terrain, and then go and do the research. And most of them don't even make it that far. The locals are not paid enough, and so there's no incentive for them to hang out in a remote mountain village for six months of the year, in 18 feet [5 metres] of snow and track – what? I mean, we've had trackers who've gone out of their hut, gone 50 paces and come back and said, 'Oh there are two snow leopards here.' Well, they've not made that effort and we've found that they weren't snow leopards to begin with; they were wolves or something else.

People coming from the West, when they arrive in Pakistan, the problem they face is that, by the time they've gone through the whole system, arrived at the place, gone through the local politics and the issues, they've really not had the opportunity to go out in the field and do stuff. Most of their time is taken up in the politics of things, in just developing their status and their place in the organization.

There's a lot of politics in organizations like that, especially at grass roots, especially in places like Chitral, where the local bigwigs and some organizations have their own agendas and use the poor locals to their advantage, which has nothing to do with the animals or their well-being. The animals are probably something that these people from the West, the scientists, never even get to see. They probably stay there a year or a year and a half and come away with some photographs that someone else took. So technically, their accessibility if you like, is zero. So what are they going to research on? Speculation maybe – you know, bits and pieces of information, second-hand information. It's well meant, and it's probably going to get there, but it hasn't got there as yet.

NISAR MALIK

The environmental movement, I consider, has got it wrong because right at the beginning they started out with wonderfully liberal good intentions. I know because I was part of it way back then. But, like all human-group movements, as they grow bigger their quality tends to diminish. It's almost as if the quality of a movement was at the highest common factor of its members, and the more members that you have in it the lower that factor gets.

In many ways, the green movement has suffered from the same kind of problem that the trade unions have. I know them well; I grew up with them because my family were involved in the movement. It was wonderfully altruistic and well intentioned at the beginning, but as they grew bigger and got more and more power, inevitably they became corrupted to an extent – not all of them, but some of them. And the same kind of process is happening with the green movement.

JAMES LOVELOCK

I work an awful lot with organizations like WWF, who will launch a campaign and say, 'Right, in 18 months we're going to save the seas.' Or with the World Bank, which says, 'In five years' time we're going to eradicate poverty.' And that's a load of baloney, because it doesn't work like that. Human beings don't work on timescales like that. We had a meeting recently where we brought together religious leaders with political leaders. At one point, when they were all talking about the millennium development goals which are set for, I think, 2015, one of the Taoist monks from China stood up and said, 'You know, the problem is, we don't think like this. We think in generations.'

And although at one level, that drives people like me slightly crazy, because I'd love to see things sorted out now, actually there's a great deal of wisdom in that. People do not change overnight, or if they do, very often it's

I think what the faiths know is that if you're going to do anything and you're going to do it for a long time, it takes a long time to root

almost all the major ecological crises of the world need mathematicians, psychologists, philosophers and economists as well as biologists working on them

like the parable of the sower: it may spring up quickly, but it hasn't got roots. I think what the faiths know is that if you're going to do anything and you're going to do it for a long time, it takes a long time to root.

For example, we developed with the Jews an environment festival based on a festival that already exists – Tu Bi'Shevat, the Festival of Trees – and this means that every single year Jews all round the world celebrate the environment. They think about tree planting, they think about the environment, they have environmental programmes. And it's not just going to be for three years. That's now engrained into Judaism. It will be going on – God willing – for the next 200 or 300 years. That's how change happens. **MARTIN PALMER**

I think a rather tunnel vision of the kind of ways in which we might get out of the difficult situations we're currently experiencing has been a problem as well – a belief in management solutions.

I would favour a much broader, multidisciplined, humble investigation of the big ecological problems in which we are engaged, not single-channelled, simply scientific ones. Almost all the major ecological crises of the world need mathematicians, psychologists, philosophers and economists as well as biologists working on them. **RICHARD MABEY**

Putting It Right

9

There are 6 billion people in the world, and about half of them are living in poverty. Ideally, all humans should have access to basic necessities, but can that be achieved without further plundering the Earth's ecosystems? Some people think so, some merely hope so and some have some reasonable and even ingenious solutions.

All the poor countries and the poorest people are entitled to develop and have more material goods. And there are still nearly a billion people who are hungry. About the same numbers don't have clean water, half of humanity doesn't have sanitation and so on. I think that when the early environmental movement said, 'Stop all development,' it paralysed the world. We've polluted and plundered it, now let's pull up the ladder behind us, and the rest of the world can stay impoverished and in need. That just won't do. So we have to say, 'Yes, everyone is entitled to the basics of a decent life.' Therefore the poorest countries and the poorest people are entitled to economic growth and development and access to technology that they haven't got.

The only way we can manage this is not by saying that everyone keeps growing. Anyway, as things are, the rich are getting richer, and many of the poor are getting a little bit better off, and some are getting poorer. So we have to say we're going to make the world more equitable. Everyone's entitled to the basics. It's not economic growth for economic it's not economic growth for economic growth's sake, it's a more equitable world where everyone has the basic things that human beings need

growth's sake, it's a more equitable world where everyone has the basic things that human beings need.

We cease to find the meaning of life out of more and more economic growth and more and more consumption. Where that's happening, it's not only plundering the world and is unsustainable, it's making people miserable – obese people, people consuming too many drugs and too much alcohol, mental illness, family break-up, lack of friendship. It's also unsustainable for the planet. I think the OECD country model of society now is an ugly, unhappy one that doesn't fulfil what human beings really need. **CLARE SHORT**

It's become one of the classic stand-offs in discussion of this issue to say that somehow there's a conflict between dealing with poverty and respecting the environment, and I think in the short term, that may often feel as if it's true. You need to increase food production at a very rapid rate, and you need to cut some corners. In the long run, however, it seems absolutely clear that this has to be a fallacy.

An exploitative attitude to the environment is something that advantages the better-off and disadvantages the poorer. It's something that reduces the entire capital of the globe. It's something that represents an attitude to those without power and leverage in the world, which is I think deplorable.

So the medium-term question is: how do we make sure that the corners we may cut or the risks we may take in economic development, in moving people out of poverty, are compensated for or balanced by positive proactive measures in other ways?

ROWAN WILLIAMS, ARCHBISHOP OF CANTERBURY

Very often people create a false dichotomy between industrial and economic advancement and environmental well-being. The two can go hand in hand. It reminds me of a great cartoon I saw the other day that depicts two cavemen sitting on the ground having a conversation. One caveman says to the other, 'I don't understand. All our food's organic, our water's pure, our air is clean, we get plenty of exercise, but nobody lives past 30.' It's exactly the way it is. Modern industrial advancement and economic growth lead to a lot of the simple environmental benefits that we in the United States take for granted. They simply don't exist in the developing world – benefits such as medical advancements, schools, clinics and potable water. These are things that are a part of everyday life here, but they're things that are products of our industrial revolution, something that's never happened in the third world.

If you look at particularly how the United States has progressed over the past three decades, for instance, emissions of our six principal pollutants have decreased dramatically, while at the same time our Gross Domestic Product has increased. Take the problem with the ozone layer for example. The United Nations acknowledges that due to a reduction in CFCs worldwide, the ozone layer is repairing itself and should be on that course through 2050. The argument that industrial activity does not mesh with environmental stewardship and sound environmental well-being – I just don't see it.

I think 'sustainable development' is a very clever term that's been created by the environmentalists. It's sustainable, it's development; how could anybody be against it? But in reality what they're really promoting is no development, and that's the key. It's very thinly veiled. They don't want any development, or any development that's of any worth to the developing nations of the world. They want to put the solar panels on top of huts, the wind turbines in the fields, the inefficient things that aren't truly going to bring these people out of the energy dark ages and help them progress as a people.

it's sustainable, it's development; how could anybody be against it? But in reality, what they're really promoting is no development

It's important that we identify what the real environmental problems are. There are many environmental problems that don't get talked about these days. I'm talking about bringing electricity to masses of people efficiently and cleanly. I'm talking about potable water, clinics, health care and eradicating diseases and pests such as mosquitoes which can carry malaria. These are environmental catastrophes that oftentimes are exacerbated by some of the environmental policies that first-world organizations are pushing. **PEYTON KNIGHT**

We have to recognize that there is more and more demand for ecological goods and services, such as energy, clean water and biological resources. The challenge is, how do we meet that demand with a minimum footprint on our environment? **ROBERT WATSON**

Is sustainable development the answer?

For me, sustainable development is the most powerful idea ever invented. It's about protecting the Earth's natural capacities at the same time as meeting human needs. That sounds quite a simple and straightforward idea, but it's incredible how difficult that is to get across into the mainstream policy-making process, where pretty much all the time it's not a question of bringing these things together and doing them as a single idea but trading them off against each other. It's either the environment or people. And if we're going to solve these big problems like the mass extinction that's taking place and the climatic change that poses so many dangers to people, we have to do away with that false choice. It's not a question of the environment or people. It has to be both, and that's what sustainable development is all about.

> sustainable development is the most powerful idea ever invented. It's about protecting the Earth's natural capacities at the same time as meeting human needs

Most of the examples of sustainability and sustainable living that we can see in the world are in traditional societies. For example, the rainforest people are still living in relative harmony with the ecosystems that have sustained them for many thousands of years, and those organized societies that have lived in that way have done this quite consciously. They've understood the limits that they have to respect in terms of how the ecosystem will meet their needs, and they've invented traditions and folklore that prevent those limits being breached.

When the Western style of development finds those resources attractive, of course, then those traditional lifestyles are being replaced with the export-led, resource-hungry approaches that we see very much in the West. And a lot of those societies are, as a result, being wiped out.   **TONY JUNIPER**

Sustainable development is an essential idea and also an idea that has been badly abused. You see all sorts of activities being now defended or characterized as sustainable development, and it's important to step back and ask, what is this really about? What do we mean when we say that, and what's the essential notion here?

The key is that we have to build conservation, stewardship of the planet, into our own development. And that's what sustainable development should be about. Basically, the essential idea of sustainable development was right from the beginning: that one ought to be pursuing human development in a way that's compatible with the protection of the Earth's living systems. And I think it still has that essential meaning, although we've come to understand a lot more

> sustainable development is an essential idea and also an idea that has been badly abused

about what it requires, including recognition that, in order to make development sustainable, you need to pay attention not only to what's happening locally, in the immediate ecosystem, but what effects you're having on the planet as a whole.   **JAMES LEAPE**

Sustainable development is essential if we're going to see wildlife in Africa in the next 100, 200 years. Sustainable development is very much a possibility, but it has to be done at a very large scale. I think anyone who tries something too localized is going to be swamped by larger economic forces that are happening elsewhere in those countries. But if you have a true partnership between governments, the private sector and the local people that involves people various distances away from the reserve, and if people feel economic security, if they have ways to sustain their livelihoods without extracting their basic resources – then, yes, sustainable development is possible.

We've seen on other continents that, as people have become more industrialized, more urbanized, that the pressures on the natural world can be diminished. In Africa we're just not there yet, but we do have in some countries in Africa a very rapid economic growth. And so the idea really should be to try to channel that economic energy in ways that are environmentally friendly. If we can do things the right way, then it'll be possible to have people recognize the value of their natural resources that seem to be taken for granted right now. Wildlife is something that they live with, it's something that they are sometimes harmed by, but ultimately it's their greatest natural resource, and it grows back. We could even stand for things to get fairly bad, but they'll all bounce back. As long as the land is set aside, as long as there's habitat that is adequately gazetted and valued by the people that live next to it, then sustainable development is really the way to go, and it's the only hope in the long term.   **CRAIG PACKER**

Sustainability cannot be defined in simple terms. It is not a term that you can catch in one phrase, which is why the Roundtable on Sustainable Palm Oil needs 8 principles and 48 criteria to define it. But broadly speaking, sustainable palm oil or sustainable sugar or sustainable cocoa has been grown with respect for the environment, with protection and maintenance of as much biodiversity as possible, and has to give an adequate yield, an adequate return on investment to those who financed it. It has to provide for good and safe working conditions and good and meaningful incomes for those who work in it, and it has to satisfy consumer needs, in terms of quality, price, taste, appearance.

JAN KEES VIS

I can't define sustainable development, but I can define unsustainable development, and that is where we are adversely perturbing our environment. When we lose biodiversity, perturb the climate system, pollute our waters and degrade our land, that is clearly unsustainable in the long term. We need to integrate environmental considerations into national economic planning and energy, transportation and agricultural systems

> we need to integrate environmental considerations into national economic planning and energy, transportation and agricultural systems

and consider the consequences to the Earth's environment, to the biodiversity, and the climate system and local air quality.

We must match our need for economic development with our need to protect ecological systems because they, in the long run, underpin sustainable development and a more sustainable way of life.

ROBERT WATSON

I think the phrase sustainable development is used a bit too casually for my taste. I don't think it's literally a contradiction in terms, because if you look at a lot of natural systems you will see something very close to true sustainable development. The way in which, let's say, an open field left for 100 years turns into a complicated woodland, without any necessity for human intervention, is the most perfect model for sustainable development. A complex system developing at no cost whatsoever to the environment out of a simple system. That's what development is.

Applied to humans, I think sustainable development has become a rather empty slogan that any cheap-jack politician or industrialist will use to try to sanitize what they want to do. And, if you look very closely at ideas for 'sustainable communities', for instance – a very popular

> sustainable development has become a rather empty slogan that any cheap-jack politician or industrialist will use to try to sanitize what they want to do

term in the developed world at the moment – you will find that what is really meant is sustainable once they've been built, and even that looks a bit questionable. It's not sustainable in terms of the input of metals and raw materials, not sustainable in terms of the land, which is irrevocably taken out of green space. So, I think it's a very empty term when it's used as propaganda to try to make development look sweet. But as an energizing idea, as a way of referring human ambitions to the rigours and the demands of an ecosystem, it's useful, but it must be done with great discipline if it's to be of any value at all.   **RICHARD MABEY**

As it is now, 'sustainable development' is a contradiction in terms. We can have no kind of development – we've gone much too far. What we need is a sustainable retreat from the mess that we're now in. There's no simple answer to what should one do for a sustainable retreat. It depends where you are. If you're living in Iceland, you're exceedingly lucky because you have all the energy you would ever need from geothermal. Not only that, you may even be able to make an income exporting it, and I think this is even considered by the Icelanders. If, on the other hand, you live in a densely crowded, small group of islands such as this [the UK], you have to do different things.

We don't have any geothermal energy worth a damn, but to run a big city like London, for example, you need a constant and never-failing supply of electricity. It would only need to fail for a week, and you would see London turn into one of those refugee camps like Darfur. It would be as bad as that.

We need a sustainable source of electricity and this is one of the reasons I'm so pleased the Government is choosing to continue to run nuclear power in this country. I'm not a nuclear fanatic, but I think it's a very safe, stable way of providing electricity for people. It's not the only way, of course. If they could do the Severn barrage, I think that would be a wonderful bit of renewable energy for this country, and they should do it.

I don't think that onshore wind farms are a good idea at all, mainly because we're going to need every bit of land we've got for growing produce to feed ourselves. It's a bit like World War Two.

we can have no kind of development – we've gone much too far. What we need is a sustainable retreat from the mess that we're now in

JAMES LOVELOCK

I think it's quite important to realize that sustainable development as a concept has only been around for about 20 years, and it is still forming itself. There is still a lot of uncertainty about it. But I do fundamentally disagree with people who say it's a contradiction in terms. Who's really going to go out there and pretend there isn't going to be development in human societies – development in the way we help poor people to live better and more dignified lives? What kind of world is it in which there's going to be no development? But that development has got to be delivered in ways that are compatible with life-support systems, ecosystems, natural services and all the rest of it. That's what we mean by sustainability.

So, far from being a contradiction in terms, sustainable development is the only way in which we're going to be able to meet people's economic aspirations without destroying their life-support systems.

JONATHON PORRITT

It depends on what you mean by sustainable. What I challenge is 'sustainable growth'. The world is a finite system. There is only enough room for a certain number of people before we start to drown in our own sewage and our own exhausts. We are already drowning in many places. So I think there is a real need for sustainable levels of contentment that people can be comfortable with.

As a species, our heads are firmly in the sand. We behave like somewhat I challenge is 'sustainable growth'. The world is a finite system. There is only enough room for a certain number of people before we start to drown in our own sewage

one spending wildly on their credit card in the belief that the bill will never come. But it's already in the mail. If we all want to have three holidays abroad, three, four or five cars, a house here or a holiday home there, and expect that that's a standard of living that will eventually be attainable for every human being in the world, we are stuffed. It's just not going to be possible.

BARBARA MAAS

Sustainable development has become this buzzword that everyone uses to mean everything. Now I'm not a development specialist. What I'd like to think about is sustainable conservation – to ask, how do you make conservation stick, really stick over the long run? And if you're going to make conservation stick over the long run, you have to build within it some elements that motivate or make better the lives of the people who can benefit from that activity. So, as a conservationist, I find a lot more clarity on what I need to think about and what I need to do in order to get a conservation project to be long-lasting, as opposed to just saying, 'Oh we're just going to do sustainable development' – a green stamp for any kind of development activity we want out there.

I don't want to imply that sustainable development isn't good if you can get it done, but development itself is pretty hard. I mean, think about how long Oxfam and Care and the World Bank have been trying to just do development, and then to add this notion of green development, sustainable development, is very, very challenging. I think brighter people than me are working on that problem. But sustainable conservation – now that seems like something worth pursuing.

To me, what sustainable conservation means is fundamentally linking people's lives with nature. Once upon a time all of us were very intimately linked with nature, right? And through development and industrialization we started losing those linkages. We still are to some extent. The water that you drink did once upon a time flow in a river somewhere. But it's hard for you to trace that linkage; whereas a woman who lives on the edge of a forest in Sierra Leone knows exactly where her water's coming from in the wet season and exactly where it's coming from in the dry season. When I think

what sustainable conservation means is fundamentally linking people's lives with nature

about sustainable conservation, I want to do the kinds of conservation projects that fundamentally give the local people a stake in what they are trying to save.

M. SANJAYAN

Does hunting still have a place in modern environmental thinking?

There's no question that hunting species in a sustainable way will continue to be part of conservation, and should be. In terrestrial systems, hunting has been a part of wildlife management for millennia. And as long as that hunting is consistent with protecting the essential integrity of those systems, it ought to be allowed.

JAMES LEAPE

Canned hunting is basically when someone has a lion that they breed up in a cage, and then they release it, and a tourist comes along and pays some money and shoots it. That's a canned hunt. Or the animal is in some way impaired or restricted. It's not a wild lion doing its wild thing, living out there.

Trophy hunting is going out there and shooting a lion which is essentially living as a lion in order to get a trophy that you then put on your wall. Trophy hunting in general, if practised properly, has been shown to have positive impacts on conservation. There is no doubt that several countries in Africa have managed their wildlife in such a way that trophy hunting has managed to bring back those populations. The same thing has happened in the United States.

So hunting can play a role in conservation, but I think it matters how the hunt is done, how that money is put back into conservation, and not going the route of canned hunts, which tend to be staged, which play very little role in conservation. I think this is an important distinction to make. **M. SANJAYAN**

Many areas here in Tanzania that are outside the protected areas are actually utilized by trophy hunters, and trophy hunters provide incentives to tolerate these kinds of animals. Areas that are not gazetted as national parks – they're not game reserves but areas where people are allowed to live – are not places that many tourists want to go to take photographs. The scenery may not always be very good, the access is very poor, brush may be thick, tsetse flies may be rampant. All of these may keep out high-volume tourism, but trophy hunters will pay a very high amount of money to be able to have an opportunity to go and hunt some of these dangerous species. Now, if they generate sufficient revenue and if they accept the responsibility as much as possible for trying to protect people against these dangerous species, then we might see protection of areas outside those that are gazetted as islands of safety.

many areas here in Tanzania that are outside the protected areas are actually utilized by trophy hunters, and trophy hunters provide incentives to tolerate these kinds of animals

We're doing these projects on mitigation, trying to reduce the conflict between lions and people, because there is a need to find ways that wildlife habitats can be extended beyond these artificial boundaries – the game reserves, the national parks. These are the hunting areas. The hunters, in many cases, are the sole protectors of those areas. They do the anti-poaching patrols, and they have the responsibility for doing community projects that engage local people and help local people become partners in conservation, change their attitude away from being mere spectators in wildlife to becoming participants.

Even right here in the area that we're filming right now, there are people working with hunting companies that have engaged the local people to tell them if there are poachers. They say, get the information to the right authorities, because those poachers are coming from other parts of the country, and they're stealing your resources. Your wildlife is at risk because of the behaviour of other people. Likewise, if there's mitigation of the conflict, if people really feel valued and they feel that their own safety does matter to the conservationists, then they become very enthusiastic partners, rather than simply looking on as if to say, why should I tolerate these animals at all?   **CRAIG PACKER**

Trophy hunting with markhor, ibex or any other wild animal in Pakistan is one of the links. It isn't the end-all answer to economic growth or creating that infrastructure – it's just one element. You have education; you have relocation of villages; you have trophy hunting; you have village shops, schools, health units, ecotourism. They all have to come together before you find the economic solution.

Trophy hunting is a greed solution, because what you're doing is you're giving $50,000 dollars to a community that doesn't get $500 through everything else that it does. You've got to put it into perspective. The average person in a national park, or on the fringes of it, would make less than $200 a year. Now, what do you expect when he sees $50,000 come in from one trophy? You've just absolutely taken his view and vision away from the big picture and focused it, and the question mark in his mind is, 'How is part of this money going to come into my pocket?' The rich locals become involved, greed overtakes the cause. So it's very difficult. Trophy hunting is not the only element. It's part of a chain, and we don't have that chain in place right now.   **NISAR MALIK**

Is ecotourism a way forward?

Ecotourism is a good activity if the project is well designed – that is, it takes into account what the footprint will be of the tourists on that area. In many respects, it buys ownership in the local community, assuming that they benefit from some part of the revenue stream. Ecotourism activities can often employ local people, either as guides or as hotel staff for the tourists, but it will depend on the exact design. The Bank has been involved in some ecotourism projects, including ones covering coral reefs, and the challenge is to make sure that the project is designed to benefit local people, and not just the national treasury, and that the footprint on the coral reef system is absolutely minimal.

Ecotourism can certainly benefit one area over another. Those areas that are highly biologically diverse and rich – say, coral reef systems or a forest that has lots of plants, animals or butterflies – will clearly be areas that attract tourists, and therefore there's no question that those areas will attract money and will be preferentially safeguarded over other regions that have less diverse flora and fauna. A key question is how do we ensure that those areas less attractive for tourism are also protected? We need to develop other arguments for protecting them.

> those areas that are highly biologically diverse and rich ... will clearly be areas that attract tourists, and therefore there's no question that those areas ... will be preferentially safeguarded

Does that forest system purify a lot of the water that is needed downstream by the farmer? Does it, or can it, provide other sources of revenue for local people living near it? One would want to assess those areas to see what are their other values. If indeed it's an area that doesn't seem particularly rich in biodiversity, doesn't provide very many ecological goods and services, it may well be an area that could effectively be converted into an agricultural site. So, in some respects it is a balance: how important is that intact ecosystem versus to what degree could it be important if it's converted. And this is where we have to assess the trade-offs.

ROBERT WATSON

Some ecotourism is returning real benefits to local communities and creating real incentives for conservation. Other so-called ecotourism is just regular tourism with a green face. The challenge for us is, over time, to make that distinction, to make sure that tourism is increasingly providing incentives to conservation and not just dressed up to pretend that it is.

Take the Amazon, for example. The government of Brazil has committed to protecting 12 per cent of the Amazon, the largest protected-areas network in the world, larger than the entire US national park system. And at the same time they are investing in assuring that there are areas throughout the Amazon that are available for sustainable use, for example, tourism. And they have been a leader in making sure that there are well-managed forests that can be used for development by local communities, in tandem with areas that are strictly protected, to conserve biodiversity. This can be a model for forests around the world.

some ecotourism is returning real benefits to local communities and creating real incentives for conservation. The other ecotourism is regular tourism with a green face

Nature conservation works best in a mosaic that has some areas of habitat strictly protected, so that the ecosystem works in its natural way. Other areas allow managed use, a limited harvest of resources – in the case of the Amazon, like Brazil nuts or heart of palm. And then there are other areas that are open to more intrusive developments. We've seen lots of evidence in the Amazon and elsewhere that that kind of mosaic can work. But you need strict protection of some habitats as a cornerstone for that broader pattern.

JAMES LEAPE

Tourism is now one of the world's largest industries. It's one of the fastest-growing industries worldwide. Therefore, the economic momentum behind it is absolutely huge. If we can find ways of turning tourism into a positive force for conservation, then I think that's all to the good. But it does embrace a very wide range of different activities, from taking the bus and walking along the coast of England right through to flying on a jumbo jet to the other side of the world, going in a four-by-four vehicle, disturbing wild creatures, impinging on local communities' peace and tranquillity. So there is an awful big spectrum in there in this idea of ecotourism.

But I think the point has to be, yes, let's harness tourism to pursue ecological outcomes, but let's do it in a sustainable way – rather than simply making this a compromise between wildlife on the one hand and people's desire to travel on the other.   **TONY JUNIPER**

I think you'd be a very pessimistic person today not to welcome the growing focus on ecotourism of one kind or another, because whichever way you cut it, it's got to be a damn sight better than the Earth-trashing tourism that has dominated the global market up until now. But it's still a very chaotic scene. You've still got lots of people making completely unwarranted claims about how sustainable or ecofriendly their tourism proposition is. I don't think we should be too upset about that. This is a marketplace that is still forming itself. Definitions are being made, standards are being set, and experience is being learned.

I feel we will arrive at a point where genuinely sustainable tourism becomes a reality for a large number of people. I don't believe ecotourism will become a reality for the whole of the current travelling population, because there just aren't enough sustainable opportunities

you'd be a very pessimistic person not to welcome the growing focus on ecotourism … because whichever way you cut it, it's got to be a damn sight better than the Earth-trashing tourism of that kind out there in the tourism business. But it will make a big difference, and it could be a very benign contribution to managing some of the worst impacts of travel and tourism at the moment.

JONATHON PORRITT

I would suspect that in every place there's a way of organizing things. Galapagos is a very good example. Galapagos is a group of smallish islands, and tourists have to visit them by boat. There's no other way. Well, there are a couple of airports, but that's all. So you can regulate where they go, and it is very well done. They go along established routes; they get permits for the boats to go to certain areas.

The visitor is unaware of the bureaucracy that lies beneath this. All he knows is that he gets up in the morning and visits the island nearby and goes to bed. The next morning, he gets up and visits a different island, because overnight they sailed to another one. And they keep visiting groups apart from one another, so that they seldom overlap and get a marvellous impression of these desert islands with their extraordinary populations of reptiles and birds. That's well done.

But at the same time there are islands to which nobody goes. These islands contain much the same creatures as those visitors can see elsewhere. But these are the protected heartlands – the precious heartlands on which the rest of the islands depend. So you have your cake and you eat it in those circumstances. **DAVID ATTENBOROUGH**

We're just starting now in Ethiopia to see the first ecotourism trips come in – people who have come specifically to see rare animals like the gelada baboon, the Walia ibex, the Ethiopian wolf. Hopefully, the numbers will grow, and we're gaining tourism money from people coming to see these animals. The question is just whether it will be in time.

The problems in the Ethiopian ighlands are so desperate in terms of poverty and land-use that this trickle beginning now is too little too late to save the animals on its own. Ecotourism will not be the answer for the Simien Mountains. It can help, and it's certainly great to see people coming to see animals in the Ethiopian Highlands, but the much bigger picture is to do with alleviating the poverty of the millions of people who live in the Ethiopian Highlands, people who will not get a trickle-down effect from the tourist dollars. Ecotourism can only really help a few locals.

In the Simien Mountains, we've been trying to get more tourists in there to see the amazing animals. It used to be a wonderful place to go trekking in. You would get your local mules, a lot of money would go to local mule drivers and guides, and you'd have to walk into these amazing mountains. The government said that a new road going right through the centre of the park would allow many more tourists to get access to this area. But what we've seen happen is tour groups that literally do not get out of their bus. We're seeing ten times the tourists come into the park, but it's buses driving up and down this road, people taking photos out of the window, turning around and heading back down to the city. And so none of that money is going to the locals anymore.

The tourist dollars would trickle down when there was trekking, but the road has just been a disaster on all counts. It's been a disaster for the animals, a disaster for the habitat, and it's been a disaster for the locals, because they now don't have the access to the tourists.

CHADDEN HUNTER

Can private ownership of land and 'green colonialism' be a solution for conservation?

I am an entrepreneur. I acquired a piece of the rainforest last year. I was fed up with politicians talking, and I saw an opportunity to actually take action, and that's why I bought it.

Having followed the debate about the environment, I have become increasingly concerned, because if we look at the changing weather patterns, if we look at how much of the rainforest has been deforested over the past 50 years, it's horrendous. The impacts, the cause-and-effect scenario here is something that troubles me a great deal, and it is something that is changing exponentially if we look at the increased activity in hurricanes, if we look at global warming. I remember being able to ski, when I grew up, from October through almost into May, and nowadays in Stockholm there is hardly any snow any more.

I have about 400,000 acres [160,000 hectares], all in the state of Amazonas. The rainforest that I bought had a forestry operation where the logging was done in a very controlled fashion, in accordance with the Forest Stewardship Council guidelines, where you can log something like one cubic metre per hectare every 20 years – so not very much. But that's not why I bought the rainforest, to keep logging. So I shut down the sawmill and stopped anything to do with cutting trees.

Is rainforest expensive to buy? Here we get to one of the core issues in the future of all environmental debate. No. Rainforest is very, very cheap to buy, relatively speaking, compared to anywhere else in the world. It would cost a fraction of the environmental-servicing costs that governments, and therefore taxpayers, would have to fund every year if the rest of the world were to pay the nations with rainforest to make them protect and preserve it.

The prevailing land value of the rainforest in the Amazon is around $20 billion. If you think about the hurricane season, which costs the insurance companies $150 billion, and you look at the direct link between hurricanes and the burning of the Amazon rainforest, just for the insurance companies

it would cost a fraction of the environmental-servicing costs that governments, and therefore taxpayers, would have to fund every year if the rest of the world were to pay the nations with rainforest to make them protect and preserve it

the payback would be very, very quick.

> the burning and
> illegal logging that
> takes place in the
> Amazon accounts
> for ... over 1 billion
> tons of carbon, i.e.,
> more than the entire
> Kyoto Protocol
> CO_2-reduction
> targets over 17 years

The impact of the burning and illegal logging is enormous. First of all we have to look at the Kyoto Protocol, which in its current format is quite meaningless. There are lots of things that are ill-defined and create confusion. And more to the point, China, India and the US, which account for more than half of the world population, are either not signed up to it or bound by it, and that is a matter of concern.

If we put the targets of the Kyoto Protocol in perspective, the burning and illegal logging that takes place in the Amazon accounts for about 3 million hectares [7.4 million acres] on an annual basis. Now, 3 million hectares stores over 1 billion tons of carbon, in other words, more than the entire Kyoto Protocol CO_2-reduction targets over 17 years, which is frightening in itself.

And there is another important issue to consider. Most of the Amazon-region states are very poor, and most of the land is owned by the local governments, and most of the illegal logging takes place on their land. And the reason is that, out of the Amazon population, 99 per cent are extremely poor. So they don't have any other choice than to do illegal logging and burning to create settlements and plant crops in order to survive. So what is needed here is a combination of careful protection and preservation of the forest and also social infrastructure programmes to offer alternatives to the poor people living in the region.

I make sure that no illegal logging takes place by having people monitor the land. But I also let the local population go onto my land and harvest Brazil nuts or acai, which is a popular antioxidant. I also let scientists do research projects, cataloguing species for medicinal purposes, to make the most of an incredibly biodiverse environment.

Is it a form of 'green colonialism'? I think it's the opposite, because what I associate with colonialism is that you buy something from poor people and then you exploit them in various forms. Here we're doing exactly the opposite. Well, at least that's what I'm doing, which is to buy land and then protect and preserve it. So I would call it 'planet rescue' as opposed to colonialism.

JOHAN ELIASCH

to buy land and then protect and preserve it ... I would call ... 'planet rescue' as opposed to colonialism

This interesting concept of 'eco-colonialism' that's cropping up a bit at the moment needs to be unpicked, because there are two kinds of eco-colonialism. One is going out there and buying great swathes of endangered habitats; and the other is trying to impose industrial Western values on other countries that are going through their own development curve. Putting money into purchasing endangered habitats in developing countries doesn't strike me as a particularly bad thing to be doing. Indeed, I can think of many, many worse ways for rich people to be using their money. And I have no particular problem about that as long as it's done in conjunction with the local government, with the local community and so on. Where I'm much more nervous is the imposition of our values, our sense of what is right in terms of management of the natural world, on other countries and other people. And I think we've got a lot to learn about working more effectively with people in other countries, so that we don't come across as this sort of new imperialist power saying, 'Well, we've learnt all there is to know about how to manage the environment, and now, you take it from us, this is how you're going to do it, too,' because by and large, they just feel inclined to spit in your eye, frankly.

JONATHON PORRITT

There are various things you can do to advance conservation, and sometimes you work with governments and help them establish major conservation areas. And there's also a certain role here for the private sector, whether it's indirectly through promoting ecotourism or more directly by acquiring some important piece of real estate. But the latter has its limitations. I mean, these are all sovereign countries and unless there is a strong conservation climate, like say in Costa Rica, that kind of thing can be misinterpreted. Even though it's a good thing to do, if it's not being done by somebody from the country, you can get some real resistance.

So buying a piece of the Amazon, setting it aside and protecting it is an important contribution, but it's only going to really contribute in the end if it becomes part of the local social and economic matrix. You really have to think about protected areas as not only being in a biological matrix but also being in a socio-economic matrix and even a political one. So you just have to be really smart about this stuff and look for your partners in the country in question and let them have as much of the lead as possible. **THOMAS LOVEJOY**

There are lots of individuals and organizations from the first, or developed, world who will go to places and buy or lease or put some kind of barrier round a chunk of land and say, 'This is for nature,' and we've seen some backlash to that. You can definitely hear that in Latin America and other places where there is this impression that the rich elite are going and buying private preserves. I think in some ways it's an unfair criticism of these individuals, because if they were going out there and buying a huge chunk of land and saying, 'Well we're going to just develop this and put a big factory there,' you won't hear a lot of complaints from that quarter. It all depends on what the ultimate goal is.

When an individual goes to a foreign country and buys some land and says, 'Look. I'm buying this because I think it's important for the heritage of the country,' and there is some plan down the road to transfer that ownership of the land into some local entity that can manage it in perpetuity, I think that's a noble thing to do. If someone's doing it purely because they want a playground, then it really shouldn't fall under conservation. So for me, I think the threshold, or the deciding factor, is who gets to keep that land ultimately. Is this something that is going to be returned to the country, for it to manage? Or is this always kept private for someone who doesn't even live there?

While the Nature Conservancy has certainly developed a name for being able to do private-land conservation deals, our main strategy is not to buy land and hold it. Our main strategy tends to be, how do you influence local landowners to take a role in protecting their land? Now, it could be with an industry like the soybean industry in Brazil. You could encourage them to protect important places in the Amazon. In Africa it could be, how do you develop a home-grown, local, land-trust movement? If the conservancy strategy is just to go out and buy important places around the world and hold them in perpetuity, I just don't think that all the resources coming in will ever, ever meet the demand of representative conservation. So really our notion is to act as a catalyst. We might do the first deal and set the model in motion. Ultimately it's a model that we want to see replicated in countries around the world.   M. SANJAYAN

The argument is sometimes made that, by pushing conservation, a country loses out. There is an opportunity cost for the country in question, which means, instead of cashing in their forests and selling the timber, a country ends up with something which is a smaller amount economically but has a long-time return. In my view it's a little bit like suggesting you sell your computer for the value of its silicon rather than have the computer, with all it can do, over a long period of time.   THOMAS LOVEJOY

> it's a bit like suggesting you sell your computer for the value of its silicon rather than have the computer, with all it can do, over a long period of time

I would say that there are many examples of the free market preserving environmental quality. There's the story of buffalo in the United States. When settlers first came, they almost wiped out the buffalo. It wasn't until there was a value placed on the buffalo – buffalo were able to be bought and sold and traded privately – that they started to increase in numbers again. It has to do with human beings having a vested interest in the environment or property. Without that vested interest, everybody treats the property like public property – that is, they litter it, they exploit it, they take every last bit of it until there's nothing left because they don't own it and they don't have to worry about whether or not it's going to be here tomorrow. That's the entire concept of private-property rights, and that's why private conservation, giving people – individuals – the vested interest in their own property is the best way to be a good steward of the environment. There are good people and there are bad people, and no system is perfect. But clearly private-property ownership is the best system that we've found so far.   **PEYTON KNIGHT**

I think private ownership of land and private ownership of nature is an important component, and it's an important mix. And if you can create incentives for private landowners, as the Nature Conservancy does, to do the right thing and to think about the common good, more power to you. It clearly has to be an important strategy. But I don't know any industry that, unregulated, finds a mechanism to honestly police and regulate itself. Just look at any business or any business venture, and you look at the role government has to play even in the pure free market in terms of regulation. So I do think there's a role for government. I don't think it's an onerous role, I don't think government should be the only vehicle by which you do conservation. In fact, if government's the only vehicle by which you do conservation, that's a lost game also. But it has to be there.   **M. SANJAYAN**

If we are going to use the resources of private individuals to conserve wildlife and natural ecosystems, it must be orchestrated in a framework, established by governments, which is clear about the priorities and clear about the long-term protection of these places. If, for example, the owner of a forest wanted to sell it to a logging company, then that obviously isn't going to be contributing to the long-term goal that we need to meet.

In the United Kingdom, we had an approach towards nature conservation that did rely on high levels of cooperation from private individuals. This is in relation to the so-called Sites of Special Scientific Interest, most of which were in private hands, belonging to farmers and other landowning interests. It was found, however, that even though these places were of interest, they were scientifically important, they were the bedrock of this country's conservation effort, they were being ploughed, they were being dug up, they were having houses built on them, they were being sprayed, they were having peat mined out of them. And that was the experience of private ownership contributing to conservation goals.

The fact is, it doesn't work, not on its own. You need both. You need people to cooperate to meet conservation goals, including private landowners, but it must be orchestrated through a governmental framework that sets out the priorities and has a legal baseline that says, 'Damage will not be done to these special places.'   **TONY JUNIPER**

> you need people to cooperate to meet conservation goals, including private landowners, but it must be orchestrated through a governmental framework

Making It Happen

10

We know what the environmental solutions are, but how do we achieve them? Is it down to politicians to make the right decisions and make conservation a priority? Can consumer choice in the marketplace force change and help save rainforests? What can the media do? And how powerful is grassroots activism in the face of huge industrial, political and economic pressure?

To make our political system work for the planet, we need a combination of things to be happening in parallel. One thing is for leaders to be showing some leadership. We now know what's going on with the climate, we now understand the deteriorating state of many of the world's ecosystems, and yet the policies don't change. Politicians continue with exactly the same approach towards developing their countries' economies that they've had for decades. That is no longer scientifically defensible, and we need political leaders to bring the long-term perspectives into short-term decisions.

We also need our political systems to be a little bit more accessible to the public. I think most people now recognize that we've got some major problems, and they want something done about it. Yet they find it very hard to express their views to politicians in ways that are going to make a difference.

And I think a lot of the political decisions that are taken in Western countries today reflect much more the interests of big business than they do the genuine willingness of people to go along with change. So, a system that's much more accessible to the public is another change that we need to make.

But I think also we need to be looking at the political ideas that parties have, and right now in a lot of the Western countries, there is just one idea: growth and competition. That's the big idea. Nobody yet is championing the cause of sustainability, and perhaps we need a political movement in countries, and indeed worldwide, that can start to bring that as an idea which people can vote for.

> politicians continue with exactly the same approach towards developing their countries' economies that they've had for decades ... we need political leaders to bring the long-term perspectives into short-term decisions

TONY JUNIPER

Politicians in this country – and it's true in the other so-called developed countries, the OECDs, the richer countries – are becoming less and less popular, and the lower voter turnout and the disillusionment with politics and the feeling that there's no principle and the sort of disgruntlement with the kind of societies we've got are all very widespread.

Now, what I'm talking about is an enormous revolution, and there have been revolutions before: the end of feudalism, the beginning of the nation-state, the birth of the welfare state, the extension of democracy. Human beings have achieved monumental historic and social change. The point is that it isn't easy, but if we don't do it, we're going to finish off our species.

We have to make the world fairer. We have to say, there's a limit to the resources of the planet. We've therefore got to reach agreement about how we share them and how we stop destroying them, in order that future generations can live.

It is impossible and unacceptable and just won't work to say to the poor of China and India, 'You can't have what we've got.' So the only

so the only way that
we can get a deal
with the people of
the world to preserve
human civilization is
to say, 'It's not any
longer going to be
economic growth for
economic growth's
sake. It's going to
be a sharing

way that we can get a deal with the people of the world to preserve human civilization is to say, 'It's not any longer going to be economic growth for economic growth's sake. It's going to be a sharing.'

We've got masses of capital. People don't know where to invest the capital. We've got brilliant technology. But this has got to be shared and made available across the world to everybody.

And then we've got to change the way we live and not go for endless increases in consumption. But everyone must have the basics of a civilized life, including basic health care. That means everyone gets education, and everyone's got somewhere to live and a decent diet and clean water, obviously, and sanitation and enough money to go to the theatre and get on the bus or whatever – the basics of a civilized life.

Beyond that then, we've got to learn a new way of enjoying music, poetry, friendship, family. What people call spirituality – just contemplating a bit more and thinking a bit more deeply about who we are and how we connect to nature. I think we can.

I think people are yearning for something like that. I don't know if we'll do it, but if we don't – I never thought I'd ever talk or think like this – the world will not be able to sustain human civilization. And of course, if we don't correct global warming within the next 30 years, it will become so chaotic and destructive that there'll be famine and death. It will be impossible to sustain the kind of population we've got in the world. There might be a few little huddles of humans left here and there, but the civilization

beyond that ... we've
got to learn a new
way of enjoying
music, poetry,
friendship, family

we have will be unsustainable.

Politics at the moment is in such poor shape: no principle, little honesty. It doesn't inspire anyone. So I don't think the change is going to come from politicians. I think actually we're going to have tragedies and catastrophes as a consequence of the way we're misusing the resources of the planet, and out of that, people will demand change. And the movements will come from underneath, not from the current elite of international politics.　　　　**CLARE SHORT**

> I think actually we're going to have tragedies and catastrophes as a consequence of the way we're misusing the resources of the planet, and out of that, people will demand change. And the movements will come from underneath

It's a really interesting challenge that confronts our politicians today. They're going to have to sell their political credo very differently from the way they've done it up until now. They're going to have to say that more is not necessarily better, that you may actually be happier by consuming less, that the quality of life is not dependent on the amount of shopping you can do in any one week. But, you know, these are all messages that people are much more responsive to than many of our politicians think.

Different calculations show that somewhere between 30 and 40 per cent of all citizens – in, admittedly, rich OECD countries – are prepared to trade off more money for improved quality of life. So we need to start working with that grain of human nature which says, 'I know I'm not happier just because I'm spending more or earning more. If I'm more stressed out and can't do what I want to do to achieve the goals that I have in life, then it's a zero sum gain for me.'

Politicians are going to have to get braver to make this message really work for them. Do we see signs of that at the moment? A little bit. A little bit. Not enough to give you real heart for the future, but a bit.

The biggest problem for our politicians is they're going to have to ask their electorates to pay something for what they've had up until now for free. And that's not an easy job, politically speaking. If someone's had something, as it were without paying anything for it, that's what they expect, is their due, their entitlement, their right. But that isn't going to work any longer. So the leadership challenge for politicians is to say, 'If you want to secure the benefits of this kind from the natural world, you're going to have to pay a real price for it because, if you don't pay the real price now, there won't be those benefits for you to enjoy in the future. So it's better to pay a proper rate, a proper price, than see the services offered by the natural world disappear altogether.'

Are politicians up for that kind of challenge? Well, you look around the world. How many of our politicians anywhere in the world have seriously thought through the implications of learning to live on a carbon-constrained, stressed-out planet? I don't know one. Well, Al Gore, former vice-president, failed presidential candidate, got the message about four years too late. Why couldn't he have done it when he was in office, you might ask yourself.   **JONATHON PORRITT**

I think it's precisely in that area that religious leaders may have most to contribute, simply because we, rightly or wrongly, don't have to get re-elected in a couple of years' time, and we're there to take a longer view. We're there to take a view that doesn't just depend on opinion polls or even on voting. So I think that religious communities ought to see themselves as trustees of questions like this. They're the people to whom these responsibilities are, in a sense, consigned.

ROWAN WILLIAMS, ARCHBISHOP OF CANTERBURY

protection of the environment cannot be handled ... in just the term of an election

Of course, politicians all over the world are concerned with short-term and immediate results in order to go to their constituency and say, 'I have delivered so I need a fresh mandate and you need to re-elect me.' But protection of the environment cannot be handled with short-term measures. It cannot be handled by a two-year plan or a three-year plan, in just the term of an election. You need to plan. Start today, and it will bear the fruit 10 or 20 years down the line. Therefore we need to de-link short-term politics and elections from the environment.

the most important thing is awareness. We refer to this huge loss of biodiversity, but how many of us are aware of this loss?

This is also the case for international organizations. They have a work pro-gramme of two years. They have a budget of two years. You cannot plan, and you cannot address the root causes of damage to the environment just on a short-term basis.

The most important thing is awareness. We refer to this huge loss of biodiversity, but how many of us are aware of this loss? We are not. When you are sick, you have a serious illness, say a cancer, you don't know that you have a cancer. You know your arm is functioning, your leg is functioning. You feel a little bit tired, but it's going on, and you don't know that you have a major sickness eating you. So you will not go to the hospital or go to the doctor or go to the drug store to buy something, because you are not aware. So we need to be aware that our lifestyle and our relation with nature are harming us, and we cannot continue like this.

Therefore I think this divide between the politician and the civil society will go, because at the end of the day, regardless of our status – international civil servant, citizen of the world – we are all in the same boat as individuals, as human beings. When you die, you will not die as an assistant secretary general – you die as an individual. So therefore you will be concerned, regardless of your role in the society. You will be concerned because you know that you cannot continue doing business as usual.

AHMED DJOGHLAF

I think the political system is capable of dealing with issues over the long term. A few examples: we have a several-nation commitment to advancing the next generation of fusion technology. That's a 50-year multi-billion-dollar investment and a long-term bet on an energy source that will have no environmental impact. So we can do that.

The political system creates wilderness areas, all around the world. We do it very well in Europe and in North America, and that's long term. So we know the political system can look at long-term issues. But they also have to be responsive to the real needs of people today. And for us to have clean drinking water, we need affordable energy. For us to have jobs and productivity, we need transportation systems that give us the mobility and freedom to enhance our quality of life. So there will always be a balance, and the balance is not just local, it's also neartime versus longterm. **JAMES CONNAUGHTON**

We tend to deal with environmental issues one at a time. Climate change, biodiversity, land degradation, oceans – and yet they are absolutely all coupled together.

One of the greatest challenges facing us today is how to address all of these environmental issues simultaneously. We deal with the issue of climate change separate from biodiversity loss, land degradation, the world's oceans and wetlands. We have separate international conventions for each of these environmental issues. The real challenge is how to look at our Earth holistically and recognize that all of these environmental issues are intertwined, that the threats and the drivers of change are similar for climate, biodiversity and land degradation.

> the real challenge is how to look at our Earth holistically and recognize that all of these environmental issues are intertwined, that the threats and the drivers of change are similar

The major transition we have to make is how, both at a global and at a national level, to deal with these issues holistically. How to mainstream all of these environmental issues into national economic and sector planning, which means we have to rethink the way that governments manage. Governments have departments of energy, agriculture, water and environment. These government agencies need to work together collectively to understand the challenges that sectors such as energy and agriculture have on the environment.   **ROBERT WATSON**

Can multinationals be responsible for the environment?

The truth is that, no matter what the conservation movement does, there are some huge forces that sometimes tend to line up, at least in local situations, against what conservation is trying to do: massive agriculture, like the palm-oil industry in Asia, where you can have a monoculture dominating a landscape, reducing the rainforest to essentially small chunks. It's a huge challenge.

you know you are not going to hold back the tide, but you certainly might be able to direct it

I think your best bet in trying to move forward in terms of conservation in that kind of environment is to engage with that industry in such a way that the expansion of that activity is limited, at least to the lands which are least important for conservation. You know you are not going to hold back the tide, but you certainly might be able to direct it.

                                                                 M. SANJAYAN

Well, one of the most depressing things about going back to places after you haven't been there for several years is to see how some have changed. Going back to Borneo was particularly difficult. We drove through countless miles of palm-oil plantations. As far as you could see in every direction, there was palm oil. And it was particularly disturbing when you saw oil palm that had only recently taken the place of rainforest, where some of the rainforest trunks were still left. But just to see so much of it, for the length of our drive from the airport to our filming location, is very depressing and almost brings tears to your eyes when you know what it once was.   **HUW CORDEY**

Oil palm is a plantation crop that's being grown across many tropical countries right now, and it produces large quantities of very cheap vegetable oil. This is then traded in global commodity markets and finishes up in a wide range of products: bread, soup, crisps, lipstick. A wide range of everyday goods that you'll buy contain palm oil. Now, the problem is that this particular crop grows where the tropical rain-forests grow, and in countries that are expanding the acreage of palm oil, the rainforests are being cut down. In particular, right now, across Borneo and Sumatra, very large areas of rainforest are being hacked away, the timber sold and the land planted up with palm-oil plantations. This of course is having devastating impacts on biodiversity and is also leading to the abuse of some local people and human-rights violations as well. It's a very destructive trade, and yet there appears to be very little being done to control it.   **TONY JUNIPER**

if you look at the forecasted growth in demand for palm oil for consumer goods, the forecast is that between now and say the next 30 years, the growth will be about double

If you look at the forecasted growth in demand for palm oil for consumer goods, the forecast is that between now and say the next 30 years, demand will about double from what it is now. The total area of palm-oil plantations in the world is roughly 10 million hectares [24.7 million acres] at the moment. Total production is roughly 30 million tons. So the average yield per hectare per year is three tons. But the best plots of land already make seven to eight tons per hectare per year, and the best experimental plots make ten tons per hectare per year. So if the growth in demand is expected to be twice what it is now, we would expect that you could easily meet that within existing plantations.   **JAN KEES VIS**

We've been encouraging big UK importers of palm oil to join the so-called Roundtable on Sustainable Palm Oil. This is a way of helping consumers of palm oil get products that are coming from less damaging sources – for example, locally managed areas of long-standing oil-palm plantation, compared to new areas of plantation where the rainforest is being cut down. There is a difference in the production side and therefore a difference in the environmental impact. If we can certify that, then the countries that are exporting can get the benefit, and consumers can know that they're not contributing inadvertently or unnecessarily to the destruction of these hugely important ecosystems.

so all these things we do, in the end, need an underpinning of legislation set by governments for minimum standards

The trouble is, not many companies are in the roundtable process yet, and there appear to be very few supplies of genuinely sustainable palm oil that they could be sourcing. So we've got a huge long way to go. And at the same time as these kinds of industry initiatives, which are pretty much voluntary, we do need a governmental framework. Because if 500 companies are importing palm oil into the UK, and 6 of them join this round table to have more sustainable palm oil, well very good for those 6 – it's making a contribution – but it's not going to solve the problem. So all these things we do, in the end, need an underpinning of legislation set by governments for minimum standards, because if we don't have that and everything's down to the free market and competition, there will be only a very limited contribution that can come from voluntary initiatives.

TONY JUNIPER

In the Unilever sustainable-agriculture programme that I'm responsible for, we started to look at deforestation more than ten years ago. So we have, together with WWF, started to set up the Roundtable on Sustainable Palm Oil, which was established in 2004 as a multi-stakeholder initiative. And in the roundtable we have worked on a set of principles and criteria for sustainable palm-oil production.

Deforestation, in the context of establishing new plantations, was one element that we looked at, and the members of the roundtable –

more than 140 companies and organizations already – have agreed that, for establishment of new plantations, we will no longer convert any high-conservation-value forest. The mission of the roundtable is to promote the production, procurement and use of sustainable palm oil. In order to do that, we need to define what we mean by sustainable palm oil. And in order to do that, we need to balance the interests of those trying to conserve nature, the interests of those whose livelihoods depend on the production of palm oil and the interests of those who use palm oil, put it in their products and sell it to consumers. And that is why the roundtable is a multi-stakeholder initiative. The first year of the roundtable has been dedicated to making it explicit, in eight principles, what we all mean, together, by sustainable palm oil.

The aim of the roundtable is, indeed, to try to keep any further expansion to a minimum. And if expansion is a response to demands in the market, and if demand in the market only comes from use of palm oil in consumer products, we think that you can meet the growth in demands for consumer products easily within existing land used for palm oil. If, however, the energy market also opens up for palm oil, then the situation will change dramatically.　　　**JAN KEES VIS**

This is an instance where the pressure to create renewable fuels, like bio-fuel and palm oil, has created a demand that actually degrades rainforests – as rainforests are cleared to create palm-oil plantations. But one thing is for certain: the world, especially the developing world, needs energy. Now where's it going to get that energy? If it's going to get that energy from bio-fuels and palm oil, then you're going to increase that demand and you're going to have people going in and razing rainforests in order to cultivate palm oil. But by the same token, we need to understand exactly where we want to get our energy from, and what is the most efficient and what has the least environmental impact. In a

> if it's going to get that energy from bio-fuels and palm oil, then ... you're going to have people going in and razing rainforests

lot of cases you'll find that a lot of the environmental solutions for renewables such as wind, bio-fuels, etc, have negative environmental impacts.

PEYTON KNIGHT

When you take a big issue like palm oil, where there is a huge amount of accelerated destruction going on now as the markets grow, as the uses for palm oil increase – for energy as well as for food purposes – you think, well that's a nightmare, there's just no solution. But there is a solution, of course there is.

If we were paying the real price for the benefit that we'd derive from that natural resource, from those palm-oil plantations, and we were factoring in as part of that real price, loss of service, loss of functions, loss of biodiversity, loss of all those natural qualities that we depend on, then we wouldn't be paying the ludicrously low price that we're paying for palm oil now.

JONATHON PORRITT

if we were paying the real price for the benefit that we'd derive from that natural resource, from those palm-oil plantations, and we were factoring in as part of that real price, loss of ... all those natural qualities that we depend on, then we wouldn't be paying the ludicrously low price that we're paying for palm oil now

The current green thinking is that it's only by renewable energy, including bio-fuels, that we can save ourselves and that we've got to stop burning fossil fuels altogether. I think that is horribly misplaced. It's much too late to do anything like that. Probably if we stopped all fossil-fuel burning in the world now, if we could do it by magic tomorrow, it would make very little difference to the outcome. We don't seem to realize that we've already so damaged the Earth that it's committed to major change, anyway, which will take thousands and thousands of years to recover from. So I say to the greens, 'Don't think that's the answer. But much worse than that, for heaven's sake, don't propagate the idea of bio-fuels. Don't you realize that we've done enough damage to the Earth trying to feed ourselves and to take timber from the natural forests to build our homes and make furniture with? If we try as well to take down the natural ecosystems for fuel plantations, we will destroy things even faster.'   **JAMES LOVELOCK**

Biodiversity is an ethical value I would agree, but the right for people to develop a livelihood is another ethical value that needs to be put in the balance with that. The Convention on Biological Diversity clearly states that nations have the sovereign right to decide how they want to manage their natural resources. The rainforests in Indonesia belong to Indonesia, not to Europe.

Agriculture and biodiversity cannot live side by side, by definition. Wherever there is agriculture now, there was biodiversity in the past. The point is, we have 6 billion people on this planet, the number will grow to 9 billion, and those people need to be fed. To feed them, we need to convert some nature to agriculture – we have no choice. Where we do have a choice is to decide where we do it. Not all regions are suitable for all crops. So within the regions that are suitable for a certain crop, you need to look for those areas where you destroy the least biodiversity. But as a species, if we want to survive, if we want to feed the people on this planet, we need to grow crops. It's what we have to do. The first comment we get when we Europeans go to Malaysia and Indonesia to talk about sustainability and biodiversity and palm oil is: 'Permanent forest cover in Europe is less than 5 per cent, but permanent forest in Malaysia is more than 70 per cent.' Now admittedly they include palm-oil plantations in permanent forest cover, but of the 70 per cent permanent forest cover in Malaysia, maybe 20 per cent is palm oil. So they honestly say, 'We take better care of our forests than you in Europe have ever done of yours.'**JAN KEES VIS**

If you were a shopper and you wanted to go out and buy sustainable palm oil, you would have an exceedingly challenging job even identifying which products have got the palm oil in them in the first place. Very often it's labelled generically as vegetable oil. So you don't really know whether you're buying palm oil or not, let alone whether it's coming from a sustainable source. And that leads to the conclusion that you can have as many consumer labels as you like, but the complexity in the end is going to be absolutely defeating. What you need is a legal underpinning for all companies engaged in these kinds of trades to be sourcing their products' sustainability. They do it for health and safety, why don't they have to do it for the environment? **TONY JUNIPER**

In Switzerland a cooperative retail chain introduced margarine with palm oil that came from sustainably certified palm-oil plantations. And for a while, they put a little sticker on the margarine tub that said, 'This product does not destroy the rainforest.' After three or six months, they took it off because nobody showed any interest in this sticker at all. Should the label have been more explicit and said the product came from a once-pristine forest that has now gone?

It is very difficult indeed to imagine what kind of message you could put on a product that denies the negative, whereas we all know that the negative has happened. Wherever there is a palm-oil plantation now, there was rainforest once. Wherever there is a wheat field in northern France, there was an oak forest once. Wherever there is a potato field in the UK, there was an oak forest once.

Wherever there is agriculture now, there was forest once. That's how it is, that is the footprint mankind has on nature. **JAN KEES VIS**

Can consumer choice really make a difference?

I think that the citizens of the world, including the citizens of the United States of America, are more and more aware about the damage and the consequences and the impact of the degradation of the environment in their day-to-day life. And our study will demonstrate that, for example, the citizens of the world are ready to pay a higher price for a product provided that the product is environmentally friendly. Therefore governments know that they should encourage more and more environmental products. Likewise, a number of companies have realized that the future of business is green, and if they want to invest in tomorrow, they need to be environmentally friendly in their operations. So these will lead of course to pressure from the people. And unless pressure comes from the people, the governments will tend to do business as usual.

As long as we, as citizens, continue to buy and to create markets for environmentally unfriendly products, the private sector will continue to produce these goods. So we, as citizens, say, 'We don't want this. I will not put my dollar in a product, whatever product, which is not environmentally friendly.' Do you believe that the private sector will continue marketing products that will not be sold? So we also have a responsibility as citizens to change, and to make the decision-makers change their positions because, at the end of the day, we are responsible for our lives.

AHMED DJOGHLAF

A lifestyle change is going to occur through inspiration. Fifteen years ago, none of us would have imagined that we'd be emailing at the rate we are today and having all these gadgets of interactivity, whether it's BlackBerries or video games or all the other tools – cell phones with pictures. The same thing will happen in terms of our energy utilization. As we see new home systems, soft solar panels for roofing tiles, as we see new ways of more efficient video-watching like flat-panel monitors – those are the things that will inspire consumer choices, and we need to follow those pathways, because that's the power of the marketplace. It is a fact that people now are ready to embrace new, cleaner, leaner, personal choices, but those products have to deliver better outcomes than what preceded them. And that's where we need to be focusing our efforts – driving consumers towards those choices that are smart for today and smart for the future.

JAMES CONNAUGHTON

A key question is, does the Western lifestyle have to change to become climate friendly? I'm a technological optimist and believe that we can design and implement technologies so that we can use the same amount of energy today or even more, but it will be produced and used in a much cleaner fashion, i.e., more environmentally friendly.

There's no reason why we can't transform cars to be almost zero polluting. We can use fuel cells and change to a hydrogen economy, although we have to decide how to produce the hydrogen in a sustainable manner. It could be produced from nuclear or solar power, or from fossil-fuel power, if the carbon dioxide is not allowed to escape to the atmosphere. At the same time, we waste a lot of energy. People leave electric lights on and have the thermostat set higher in winter than they do in summer. Therefore, people need to understand that we can reduce our consumption of energy without significantly changing our lifestyles.

ROBERT WATSON

The most important thing is to make connections between consumers' choices in the market and ecological impacts on the ground. For example, ten years ago, WWF formed a partnership with Unilever, which was then the largest seller of frozen seafood in the world. We were brought together by shared interests in the future of the world's fisheries. For WWF it was a concern about the health of the oceans, for Unilever it was a fundamental economic concern about the sustainability of its own supply. Would there be fish to sell 30 or 40 years from now? Those two organizations, an NGO and a multinational corporation, came together to create the Marine Stewardship Council.

And what the now independent Marine Stewardship Council does is certify fisheries that are well managed. It says to a fishery, 'If you manage your fishery in a way that ensures it will be healthy for the long term, and that the ocean will be healthy, we will allow you to use this label on your fish that tells the consumer your fishery is well managed. And consumers will start to prefer your fish over other products.'

what we need to do is to enable everybody to buy a green product without thinking about it

Ten years later, this is happening. The MSC has now certified about 4 per cent of the global supply of seafood. And MSC-certified fish are now preferred by some of the largest retailers in the world – like Wal-Mart. So you can already see that change is beginning to happen, and that change in the marketplace is directly driving conservation action in the world's oceans. **JAMES LEAPE**

Consumer labelling can be one tool that can help people choose greener products compared to those produced more destructively. But what we would like to see is no need for eco-labelling. We'd like people to be able to go into the shop and buy wood that they know is coming from sustainable sources without having to pick between different products, to choose products that have got palm oil in them, knowing full well that there has been no damage to the environment. Now, that's obviously still a long way off, but I think if we go down the route where we're going to be relying on consumer choice to be advancing these environmental goals, we won't get to where we need to get to in time. Only a minority of people go into the shop and seek out things which have been produced in a green way. What we need to do is to enable everybody to buy a green product without thinking about it. **TONY JUNIPER**

What role can the media play?

I think the media will have a really important role in conserving wildlife in the future. If you look back at the history of wildlife film-making from the very beginning, undoubtedly the awareness that has risen over the years and the introduction of animals to people is phenomenal. And with every generation we are showing people new animals – the Walia ibex in *Planet Earth* is a classic example of an animal that most people have never seen. And when you are fortunate enough to attract the size of audiences we have done through *Planet Earth*, there's no doubt that awareness has been substantially increased.

The counter-argument is that people become blasé. People see these beautiful images and don't see the problems. But luckily we're not just making programmes like *Planet Earth*; there is a range of different programmes dealing with the problems as well. And the combination is vital in conservation globally. **ALASTAIR FOTHERGILL**

You can get very mixed messages from working on *Planet Earth*, because you travel to some incredible places, but you also see a lot of destruction. But what is interesting is that there are large areas that are intact and, in some cases, virtually uninfluenced by people. And it's easy to forget that these places exist. We think we live in a very small world, but we don't. We live in a very large world – it only feels small because of the speed of communications.

I went to a patch of forest in an enormous stretch of forest in Guyana in South America. We went upriver for

we live in a very large world – it only feels small because of the speed of communications ten days, and we didn't see anybody – 250 miles [400 kilometres] of this river system had no humans on it whatsoever. And in four weeks, I saw no other people whatsoever other than those I was with. I think that's quite surprising, especially in rainforests, where you know much has been fragmented. It's good to know that there are still large patches of forest – very large, wildernessly large areas of rainforest. And it makes you feel optimistic that, while we may have destroyed an awful lot, it's not too late to save some amazing places.　　**HUW CORDEY**

While it's not our remit to make campaigning films, I believe virtually everyone who's involved in the wildlife film-making industry does it because they're desperate to raise awareness and promote conservation in the natural world. As modern society has moved away from hands-on experience with wildlife, I think a lot of people rely on natural history films as their one window into this outside world. Therefore, we carry a huge responsibility to inform and raise awareness of these various situations.

people have been turned into passive voyeurs of nature rather than engaged participants in cohabiting with nature

MARK BROWNLOW

I don't have any doubt at all in my own mind that all the programmes, radio and TV, that have been made about the natural world over the past 30 years have had an incredible impact on people. They really have. And they've helped people to understand our part in the natural world, to get a feel for its beauty, its diversity and so on. So a big tick in that box, a very positive impact if you like.

But there's also a downside to that. I think people have been turned into passive voyeurs of nature rather than engaged participants in cohabiting with nature. I sometimes think that natural history programming has left people with a sense that it's all OK out there, and look, if it's on the box, it must be fine, and it'll be fine tomorrow. When, in fact, even as the programme-makers have been out there capturing this stuff on film, they know that it's disappearing under their very eyes, and that message has not come through strongly enough from the natural-history programme-makers over those years.

JONATHON PORRITT

I don't think you will ever persuade people to care about the natural world unless they are aware of what it is that you're dealing with. Fifty years ago, nobody cared twopence about whaling, for example. It was only the underwater pioneers, people like Cousteau, who started the movement, and many distinguished underwater film-makers subsequently, who revealed what whales are – amazing creatures, the biggest creatures that ever existed, that care for their young, that undertake great migrations – sentient animals that can certainly experience pain. Most people have only seen those things on television – there was nowhere else they could do so. They didn't see them in the cinema. Where else were they going to see them? Suddenly there's a worldwide movement that says 'Save the whale. It is appalling that we should kill animals for things that we can get perfectly well in other circumstances without endangering any species and without the extreme cruelty of many of the methods of whaling.' Had it not been for people like Cousteau and the film-makers that followed him, I don't think there would be such a movement.

> had it not been for people like Cousteau and the film-makers that followed him, I don't think there would be such a movement

DAVID ATTENBOROUGH

There was a survey recently by a famous US institution saying that 97 per cent of the population are not aware of the damage that we are doing to Mother Earth – 97 are not aware! Eighty-seven per cent of policy-makers are not aware of the impact on the biodiversity of the planet. And what is surprising is 57 per cent of the educators, the teachers, are not aware. So we have a huge awareness campaign to undertake in order to demonstrate to everybody in the world that our

> eighty-seven per cent of policy-makers are not aware of the impact on the biodiversity of the planet

actions are not sustainable and we are harming ourselves by destroying the capacity of Earth's ecosystems to provide the kind of services that are vital for our survival and vital for the survival of our children. So we applaud the BBC and other media because you bring the message, the message that business as usual and the way that we have acted, at least for the past 50 years, is not sustainable and we need to change our attitude.

AHMED DJOGHLAF

What we need is more responsible media. A series such as *Planet Earth* is wonderful. It makes it possible for people to become interested in something, to become passionately concerned, and then to carry through and do something.

ROGER PAYNE

Can ordinary people change society?

One of the things that really astonishes me about Tanzania is that 38 per cent of the country has been set aside as some form of natural resource area, whether it's a wildlife area or a forest reserve – 38 per cent. It's the highest of any country in the world. A lot of those areas, though, have a status that allows people to live alongside the wildlife or in the forests. But every year in Tanzania, parts of those low-status areas are being elevated to a higher conservation status.

A game-controlled area where people are allowed to live becomes a game reserve where people are excluded. We're also seeing game reserves being upgraded to national parks, where not even trophy-hunting is allowed. So we're seeing trends towards greater protection that are driven at a grassroots level.

As people succeed in working successfully with local people to engage them in this partnership for conservation, they'll say, 'We need to protect this area. It's part of our heritage, too, and we want to see this have the highest conservation status possible.' So I think it's possible that in the next few hundred years, if economic activity continues, if urbanization continues, if people's family size slows down, you might actually see an archipelago of protected areas becoming connected, so you have what would be like a larger conservancy. I do think that's possible. If I was a gambling man, I wouldn't bet a whole lot on it, but I think it's possible.

CRAIG PACKER

as people succeed in working successfully with local people to engage them in this partnership for conservation, they'll say, 'We need to protect this area. It's part of our heritage, too

The Green Belt Movement is a grassroots environmental organization that started in 1977. But the idea goes back to 1972 and 1973, when UNEP was first created. Its main focus is to empower, especially women, to do something about the environment in which they live and, in the process, improve their livelihoods.

Perhaps the miracle of the Green Belt Movement is also its challenge, because most development agencies start at the top, and they hope that, according to the trickle-down theory, some benefits will get to the grassroots. But here the top is very thin, and the bottom is very wide. What the Green Belt Movement did was start from the bottom and try to reach the top, to influence the decision-makers at the top and to influence the grassroots people who are the main victims of environmental degradation.

It is wonderful to do it this way. It's the best way to develop, but it requires a conscious effort and a deliberate effort by governments to reach out to the people, to want to assist their large grassroots people to rise up, to support them, to encourage them. It also requires a lot of understanding by the grassroots that they need to do things for themselves, that they cannot expect governments or aid agencies to do things for them – and that requires extensive education and a lot of patience to work with them. I feel that what we have done with the

it isn't the environment or people. It's us living in our environment respectfully, happily and sustainably on this beautiful Earth of ours

Green Belt Movement is demonstrate that it is possible and desirable to start from the bottom, but the top must also be willing to work. I hope this will continue to be the norm, not only here in Kenya, but throughout Africa.

WANGARI MAATHAI

Someone once said to me that the difference between socialists – no-one talks about socialists any more – and environmentalists or greens is that socialists love people and greens love trees. I'm sure it's a stereotype. I'm a love-people person, but I honestly think if you love people, it extends. You want to be kind to animals, you want to love nature that we live amongst, and you want to care for it so that people everywhere will be OK and future generations will be okay. So I think if fuses. It isn't the environment or people. It's us living in our environment respectfully, happily and sustainably on this beautiful Earth of ours.

CLARE SHORT

Optimism and Hope ⑪

When it comes to predicting the future, environmentalists – probably more than any other group of people – have a reputation for gloom and doom. So it might be surprising to hear how hopeful so many of them are. And that's mainly because so many other people finally seem to be paying attention.

I've always felt a kind of very deep, gut-wrenching sense of pain when I think about the speed with which we're laying waste the planet; and it is a deep, emotional response to what I see is horrifically irresponsible, unthinking, unnecessary behaviour on our part. But I've always taken that kind of emotional pain and turned it into, I hope, more constructive approaches to try to deal with these things. Because if all you can do is get stuck on your personal pain, you'll never turn that into campaigning passion to put right what is going wrong at the moment. I also know that the instinct we should really rely on to persuade people to change their behaviour is not really their feeling of guilt or their feeling of fear or anger. All of that negative stuff only takes you so far. Ultimately, we have got to find a way of connecting

> ultimately, we have got to find a way of connecting people into the positive energy behind sustainability, behind environmentalism

people into the positive energy behind sustainability, behind environmentalism. And that means that while we continue to pay witness to that terrible damage that we're doing, we've got to turn people's minds towards more positive images of the good that we can still do to help protect the natural world. **JONATHON PORRITT**

In terms of changing people's hearts, one of the very powerful things is giving people nature experiences, enabling people to see the inspiration of nature first hand and taking something from that which is not very tangible, probably quite spiritual, but certainly very personal and life-changing. And if you put people in the right kind of situation, for example, to see a flock of geese on the coast in winter or to witness the emergence of the spring flowers in a woodland in some part of the world where this is an amazing, spectacular outpouring of natural change – seeing these kinds of things does change people, and that's how you get people's hearts, to bring them close to nature.

Changing people's minds is a different process altogether. We're in that process now in some Western societies, where the scale of the problems we face is now more widely understood. There is an appreciation of the intrinsic value of nature, which is the heart bit and which is now driving people to accept the need for change. And then we're confronted with a lot of complexity about how we're going to proceed – whether we need new laws, whether it's new technology, whether we need to be travelling less or travelling differently. All these things now are very much part of the debate. And I think in terms of getting people's minds to go alongside the heart, we need public debate. We need a very open and fluid discussion about what we're going to do to get the maximum possible buy-in to the changes that we need to make. That's beginning to happen here in the UK at least, and hopefully it will start to happen in some other crucial countries, hopefully the US in the next couple of

seeing these kinds of things does change people, and that's how you get people's hearts, to bring them close to nature

years. And if we then can generate that buy-in across the public for there to be changes that are going to meet the scale of the problem, then I think we're going to start to get somewhere. I think we're winning the hearts, and we're now starting to win the minds as well.

TONY JUNIPER

The paradox of trying to get people to change now is that the more painful it is in the very short term, the better it will be for humankind. Because if we get some truly traumatic shocks to the system, to put it crudely – say we have a hurricane season in America this year that has four hurricane Katrinas rather than one – the faster that pain comes through the system, the quicker our politicians, our people, will understand the need for change. If it's all very prolonged and protracted and people can go on arguing about it and know it isn't that bad and look on the bright side and all the rest of it, then we'll see decades of prevarication, putting off the so-called 'evil day' when we have to make these changes. So whack in the pain now, in the short term, and I'm sorry to say that's probably the best hope we've got for the long term.

JONATHON PORRITT

I think we need a change of heart. I think we need to see ourselves in another kind of context. Instead of seeing ourselves as fundamentally – to use the old phrase – brains on stalks, living in this artificial world, in this bubble, we need to see ourselves as part of a system, answerable to other parts of that system, and I would say also, of course, answerable to God. Now, that's something which doesn't come easily in the Western world. I think it's absolutely imperative for anyone in a position of religious responsibility in the Western

instead of seeing ourselves as fundamentally ... brains on stalks ... we need to see ourselves as part of a system, answerable to other parts of that system ... and I would say also, of course, answerable to God

world to hammer on that theme as loudly and consistently as they possibly can.

I'd hope that, in relation to the whole question about the environment and ecology, I could help to keep open some of the really big questions, the questions about what is human nature in this. It's not just a practical problem about how we avoid disaster, but how do we imagine our humanity freshly, and I think religion has a unique perspective to offer there. **ROWAN WILLIAMS, ARCHBISHOP OF CANTERBURY**

Of course, all of our aspirations will change as the crisis grows greater, and we should look back to the experience of World War Two. Everybody's aspirations and objectives completely changed once that developed in full. We'd already grown into a fairly comfortable democracy just before the war. People were looking forward to owning a car, a television set and all the rest of it. And then suddenly, they were denied the lot. But they had other aspirations, which were to defend their country, to defend their existence and their lives, and they were much bigger and fulfilled them as much as the current ones did.

JAMES LOVELOCK

The combination of politics and science can change people's hearts. What it means is that we need to inform society about the implications of their decisions so they can think how they would like to see the world evolve. And then, through a democratic society, they can inform the politicians about the type of future they would like to see for their children and grandchildren.

> we need to inform society about the implications of their decisions so they can think how they would like to see the world evolve

I don't believe the average person is willing to change his or her lifestyle significantly. When Jimmy Carter went on television and said, 'turn down the thermostats to 65°F or 68°F and put on a sweater', it went down like a lead balloon. Basically, people are not often willing to change their lifestyles, at least not quickly. Slowly but surely people can evolve their lifestyles, but to be honest, we will have to educate them. We must also provide the technology that allows them to have the lifestyle they've got used to, but without an environmental footprint.

ROBERT WATSON

we must also provide the technology that allows them to have the lifestyle they've got used to, but without an environmental footprint

Is the environment a moral issue?

Protecting the environment is a moral issue in the sense that, when we perturb the environment, we adversely affect one part of society or another. Plus, when we perturb the environment, we adversely affect other lifeforms, i.e., the biodiversity. And therefore it is indeed a moral issue. Climate change itself is a moral issue insofar as using fossil fuels puts greenhouse gases into the atmosphere. By changing the Earth's climate, it's poor people and poor countries that are most vulnerable, as well as many ecosystems.

It is a moral-ethical issue in that, to a large extent, climate change is being caused by industrialized nations using fossil fuels, and yet it's poor people in developing countries that are most vulnerable.

The other part of the moral-ethical issue is that, what we do today to our environment has major implications for future generations – our children, our grandchildren and their grandchildren – and therefore we do have a moral obligation to be wise stewards of our planet.

It is quite clear that, in many parts of the world, we have not managed to preserve nature by just arguing about the ethical value of the biodiversity or the fact it's aesthetically pleasant. Therefore, we need to couple the arguments of the ethical, the moral reasons to protect nature, with the economic arguments for protecting nature, i.e., there's economic value in ecotourism, that a pristine forest purifies the water in that area, that there are non-forest products that can be used by local people, and so on. If we can combine the ethical considerations for protecting nature with the economic considerations, then we have a much better chance of moving foward. I honestly believe it's probably the only way we're going to move forward. **ROBERT WATSON**

I think the treatment of the environment is a moral issue. It depends really on two considerations. One is that I think all morality is about human beings trying to make better sense of the world they live in, to imprint on the world the sort of meanings that are most important, that communicate most deeply. And that means using the world, responding to the environment in a way that expresses not greed or domination but respect. And I think the way we treat the environment is inseparable from the way we treat each other in that sense.

The second is that this is an issue of justice. It's an issue of doing justice to the next generation and the generation after, and if we leave them a legacy that's irreparably damaged or in some way spoiled, reduced, then we're doing a serious injustice to our children and grandchildren.

ROWAN WILLIAMS, ARCHBISHOP OF CANTERBURY

I think almost anything is a moral issue. What you eat, what you wear – anything is a moral issue, and snow leopard conservation is no exception. If we look at why snow leopards are killed, it is for their skins, either for decorating someone's home or as a fashion item. They are also killed for their bones, for which there are herbal substitutes within traditional Chinese and Western medicines. So there are really no compelling reasons why these animals should be killed. Also, nobody needs a live snow leopard in the garden. So it's a question of whether you choose to do something that is rather immoral – namely, kill an animal for decoration purposes, for vanity, for something that can be replaced by herbs or conventional medicines. Or whether you think it is important for your personal expression to have a snow leopard in a cage in your garden. None of these reasons stand up. The world is shrinking. There are so few snow leopards left now. They are more endangered than tigers. It would be really sad if, one day, those mountains no longer had snow leopard tracks in them. **BARBARA MAAS**

I think all people have a moral duty to confront what's happening to us in the future and the inequalities of the world when they're so unnecessary. We're the first generation that could abolish extreme hunger from the world. Others have dreamed of it, and it's completely practical and possible for us. So we, the privileged who have everything, have a duty to make the first moves. Where there's lots of talk about the environment, it's kind of hectoring the poor. That they mustn't chop down the forest, that they mustn't have children, while we sit here in our excess. I think the duty lies the other way round. We are the ones who've plundered and polluted, and we're the privileged rich, and we've got to lead the way in being fairer and starting to change ourselves. And some people are thinking like that but our societies aren't yet. **CLARE SHORT**

> we've got to lead the way in being fairer and starting to change ourselves. And some people are thinking like that but our societies aren't yet

Can the world religions play a role?

The environmental problems that we face in the world at the beginning of the twenty-first century are so big and so all-embracing that we need every possible leader in society to be joining in with the process of change and putting across the solutions that are needed. And that needs to be governments first and foremost, setting the legal framework, setting the leadership role that society can respond to. It needs big corporations investing in different kinds of products and production techniques. It needs the public to be changing their behaviour and demanding that governments and corporations do more. And it requires the faith leaders, these enormously powerful movements across the world – the Buddhist faith, the Muslim faith, the Christian faith. We need their leaders, too, to be putting across the moral perspective about the need to embrace solutions to these environmental problems before it's too late. It's enormously encouraging to see all of those different people now starting to come across with a single message.

TONY JUNIPER

Well, the way that religion can contribute to the environment is that it owns a lot of the planet to start with. We estimate that the 11 major religions we work with own about 7 to 8 per cent of the habitable surface of the planet – forests, farms, urban sites, you name it. They've also either built or contributed towards, or helped run or actually run 54 per cent of all schools around the world. They produce more weekly magazines than the whole of the expanded EU, and they're the third largest identifiable block of institutional investors in the world.

So when we talk about religion, yes, at one level we can think about them preaching and teaching, because all the faiths have immensely profound statements and teachings about how we should treat nature. But they also are in the business of the environment. They actually buy, they sell, they own, and they control and they influence. And those are the ways that we try and help them to be more effective, in often rediscovering traditions of how to treat the planet that they've had for thousands of years but which, in the last 200 or 300 years, they've been told are nonsense or superstition or irrelevant or non-scientific. And so they've been rather reticent about using them.

MARTIN PALMER

One of the interesting questions in some parts of the world is what is the role of the religions and faiths of the world? If one reads through the various faiths, most of them talk about protecting creation; and most of them talk about living with the Earth. And so the role of the churches could be very powerful. For example, the evangelical movement in the US is currently starting a major campaign to make sure the issue of climate change is addressed. Evangelicals take the Bible literally, and the Bible says, 'Love your neighbour, do not hurt your neighbour – do not destroy God's creation.' Climate change is indeed hurting our neighbours, it is affecting God's creation, and so parts of the evangelical movement are starting a campaign to try to protect the Earth's climate system.

Many other religions also argue for protecting our environment, and therefore it would be great if the world's community of religions became a powerful voice, working with local communities on how to protect the environment and influence decision-makers in both the private sector and in governments, to recognize we need to protect our environment, not destroy it.   **ROBERT WATSON**

From my perspective, I don't think there is any religious influence in our areas when it comes to dealing with wildlife. Religion doesn't play any part in any sort of superstition or otherwise with these animals. I think the religion of stomach is the essence here. Religion itself? Our practices in these areas are not in conflict with animals. I mean the religion says protect animals, be kind to animals and all of that – so we don't have a conflict on religion and wildlife. But religion automatically has a cultural side to it. The cultural elements are what are inherent in those locals in those parks or in those reserves. Those need to be addressed. I don't think religion has anything to do with conserving animals, at least in our part of the world.   **NISAR MALIK**

The notion of religion becoming involved in the environment, I think, is nothing but a good thing, provided that they cure themselves – and most religions have it – of a strange concept called stewardship of the Earth. We are not stewards of the Earth – we never could be. It's sheer foolish pride to imagine that we're clever enough yet to regulate the

Earth. It is an unbelievably complex system, and we couldn't possibly take on the job. But if, on the other hand, the religions – particularly the theocratic ones that believe in a single, monotheistic god – if they would look at the Earth as God's creation and sacred and not something to be desecrated, then I can't see anything but good coming from it.

JAMES LOVELOCK

> I'm pretty critical, looking back, at how pathetically disengaged the world's major religions have been. They've just stood by and watched as our industrial juggernaut has laid waste to this astonishingly beautiful created world

I'm intrigued at the way in which there's a lot more discussion now about the spiritual dimension of environmentalism and sustainable development. It's not a new thing. For me it's been a part of my drive and passion about the environmental cause for 30 years. It always has been. So I'm intrigued to see the way now in which some of the world's major faiths and religions are beginning to understand that they have a serious leadership role – to use their teaching, their holy texts, their authority, their inherent wisdom, to draw out better messages about the responsibility of humankind, in terms of acting as stewards and all the rest of it. Is it going to come in time? I don't know. I'm pretty critical, looking back, at how pathetically disengaged the world's major religions have been. They've just stood by and watched as our industrial juggernaut has laid waste to this astonishingly beautiful, *created* world. And I'm glad they're going to be out there now raising their voice in defence of our planet, our home, of God's Earth, if you like, in a Christian sense, but I think they've left it a bit late in the day.

JONATHON PORRITT

It would be unfair to say that the world religions haven't been involved. Twenty-five years ago, as I remember very well, the WWF organised a big conference of multi-faiths – of Judaism, Islam, Christianity, Buddhism. They all got together and determined that all those religions carried within them the moral precept that they ought to care for the environment and the creatures with which we share the world. I suppose in a way the problem is that the world, by and large, has turned away from religions and they are having less effect than they did. I think as far as population is concerned – and the size of population is regarded as a major factor in our problems – the Catholic Church might have a clearer view on limiting population, which would be helpful.

DAVID ATTENBOROUGH

It's actually an issue that I've been interested in for some 30 or 40 years, and it's partly because of theological interests, interests in particularly the eastern Christian world that I developed that concern. Also, of course, you may know the Bishop of Birmingham, Hugh Montefiore, wrote extensively back in the seventies and eighties on these questions. So it's not just something that happened yesterday.

But I think there is an attitude that's been around for a lot of Christians which says (I caricature it) 'the world is here today and gone tomorrow' and being overconcerned about the world is somehow inappropriate for Christians. I think this has changed spectacularly in the past ten years, and even in the past two years. We've seen, for example, very powerful conservative evangelical voices in the United States changing their views dramatically on this, even in the last year. We've seen, in the Eastern Orthodox Church, the Patriarch of Constantinople taking an extremely forthright position on this, and coordinating some very imaginative and creative work around environmental awareness with his cruises in various threatened areas of the world. And we've also seen the Lambeth Conference and a number of other Anglican meetings in the last decade making statements about this, and we hope these are beginning to filter through to ordinary believers.

Talking just about the Church of England for the moment, we've already had an environmental audit of Lambeth Palace here and are looking at various ways of reducing our footprint, including questions about environmental compensation for air miles, because I have to travel quite a lot in this job. We also launched this spring a programme in the Church of England more widely about measuring the Church's environmental footprint. We're encouraging congregations to sign up to ecofriendly policies, and there's already a network of ecocongregations that have adopted basic rules on this, and we're hoping to be employing a new environmental awareness officer for the Church of England. So, we're pushing this at national level and at local level and trying to set a good example.　　　　**ROWAN WILLIAMS, ARCHBISHOP OF CANTERBURY**

As archaeologists, we tend to emphasize the accumulation of human success and innovation and so on. The things that we invent, the things that we go on to prosper from, but we have to remember we've lost a lot as well. We have lost this intimate relationship with the world, and most importantly, we've lost respect for the resources of the world. And we've lost religious systems that underpin this – the notion that one explains the world in view of these important cosmological relationships with animal and vegetable resources. The sad factor is the rise of large-scale religions in which humans, or imaginary human-like beings, are at the centre and which immediately negate our relationship with anything on Earth. Who cares about a snail when we have the Kingdom of Heaven to look forward to?　　　　**PAUL PETTITT**

Together with our colleagues from the Wildlife Trust of India, we made contact with the Dalai Lama's office in 2005, around April, to see if he would help us to try to tackle some major conservation problems which affect tigers, leopards, otters, foxes and so on. The key point was that the tigers are threatened by the use of furs on traditional Tibetan robes.

The Dalai Lama has taken the view, which matches ours perfectly, that you shouldn't be wearing fur at all – it is an un-Buddhist thing to wear fur. Fur, after all, is another sentient being's skin. So if you're talking to Buddhists, the Dalai Lama is, of course, the best possible spokesperson you could have. What happened was that tens of thousands of people – in response to the Dalai Lama's message across Tibet, Bhutan, Nepal,

India – ripped their furs off their *chupas*, their traditional robes. They burnt their fox hats, burnt their fur blankets. And these are extremely poor people. These Tibetans live in very harsh conditions. They have very little money. So a lot of the money they do have is put into what is considered a status item of clothing. So it's a bit like us setting fire to our car because we think it's wrong to drive cars.

And they're doing it with a huge smile on their faces. They're not saying 'Well, I guess I'd better burn this now because the Dalai Lama said so.' It is really seeing people at their very best, people taking responsibility for their actions. A lot of people didn't know their behaviour was causing any damage. Some said, 'Well, we didn't kill it, we just bought the fur' – you know that old tactic that we all use in different aspects of our lives to try to shake off responsibility. But they embraced their responsibility, and I think their behaviour really sets the standard for everybody else in the world.

I have never seen anything like this happen before. It is absolutely staggering. We heard recently that all fur shops in Lhasa have closed, which is unprecedented. The price of tiger skins has dropped dramatically, the price of leopard skins dropped down to a tenth of its former value. Nobody's buying the furs anymore. It's become unacceptable – not acceptable because it's morally wrong and un-Buddhist, because Buddhism means 'Do no harm and be compassionate.' And that does not go with wearing fur.   **BARBARA MAAS**

It's probably too easy to be critical about people arriving late at the scene, as it were, and actually we've had astonishing examples of spiritual and religious leadership going back for many years now. I think that the work the Dalai Lama has done, for instance, not just in terms of

his teaching
about the proper
relationship, the right
relationship between
human beings and
the natural world has
been a beacon of
inspiration and hope

his connecting us back into the culture and natural environment of Tibet, but the leadership that he's shown – his teaching about the proper relationship, the right relationship between human beings and the natural world – has been a beacon of inspiration and hope for many, many people for many years, whichever faith they come from. And the great thing about a better relationship with the natural world is that it does, literally, touch everybody of every faith and of none. People who feel a deep spiritual affinity with the natural world but don't have any commitment or interest in formal religions can nonetheless connect through to some of that deep spiritual teaching that is there in all the best religious traditions. Welding that together now into a positive force for good, ecumenical positive force for good, that's an astonishing challenge, and I'm sure the Dalai Lama will be at the front of that challenge.

JONATHON PORRITT

Many, particularly Christian leaders, will stand up and say that it's their role to be prophetic. I have to say that, on the whole they've been pathetic, and it has actually been the environmental movement that has been prophetic. It has been the environmental movement that has actually said, 'Oh my God. Look at what's happening.' They have done what in many faiths – for instance Judaism, Islam, Christianity – would have been done by the prophets, who stood up and said, 'It may all seem great, but it ain't.'

Of course, being prophets of doom is not terribly popular, and so the environmental movement, I think, walks a very delicate and sometimes dangerous line between giving to the faiths and to the general population a clarion call to wake up and see what's happening. But at the same time, there is a tendency in the environmental movement to say, 'It's all absolutely hopeless. There's nothing we can do.

You know, we're all going down the pan.' What I think the faiths bring to this, to help the conservationists, is to remember to celebrate. Now in the environmental movement, to have a party is almost heresy. There is no environmental songbook, is there? There's not this tradition of, you know, at the back of the bus with the beers after you've been to the environmental demo, you have a sing-along. It's just a

if you don't party, if you don't say, 'Isn't this fantastic' and if you don't, to some extent, allow nature itself to hold you and celebrate that, then you've lost the point

little bit puritanical. And what the faiths bring in is a remembrance of celebration – that if you don't party, if you don't say, 'Isn't this fantastic' and if you don't, to some extent, allow nature itself to hold you and celebrate that, then you've lost the point. Yes, you have Ramadan. Yes, you have Lent. But boy, you then have Eid El-Fitr, and then you have Easter. And so yes, the environmental movement has awoken the faiths to the fact that there is a crisis. I think the faiths can contribute to the environmental movement a sense that you cannot tell people it's all bad all the time. **MARTIN PALMER**

Are you optimistic?

I'm enormously optimistic about the prospects for us to be able to achieve positive environmental change in time. I've been working in this kind of area for enough years to have seen a lot of change already. Rivers are cleaner, air quality is better, we've got more recycling facilities, and we've reduced chemical input into the environment, at least from a lot of the major sources. We've managed to ban the chemicals causing damage to the ozone layer. An enormous level of public awareness now exists around the questions like climate change. But we've got so much more to do. We've really begun to scratch the surface now. We've begun to change some of the things that were maybe the symptoms of the environmental problem, like pollution and waste generation. We've we've now got to start looking at the real causes – not just the symptoms – that are driving these things in the wrong direction still

now got to start looking at the real causes – not just the symptoms – that are driving these things in the wrong direction still. **TONY JUNIPER**

In spite of all the gloom that I have spread in all of my answers, I do feel optimistic about the oceans, and here's why. Back in the 1850s in my country, the US, there were abolitionists saying, 'You've got to get rid of slavery' – and I'm sure there were very decent people, you know, 'pillars of society', saying, 'Are you out of your mind? Are you telling me that for some moralistic reason you're going to destroy the entire economic base of this country?' And the answer was, yes. We did get rid of slavery, thank God, and it made the US a far better country. I think that once people realize what's wrong, they move fast. They move so fast that sometimes all you can do is watch. Every person my age has lived through watching the Berlin Wall come down. And what did my country say when Berliners from both sides began dismantling the Berlin Wall? What wonderful statements did it make? They can basically be summed up as, 'Gee whiz! Wow! Look at that!' In fact, it happened so quickly that nobody in the government knew what to say. When people realize what's gone wrong and what needs changing, they will change, and they will change so fast that all you can do is watch. **ROGER PAYNE**

A bit of me is pretty optimistic about the future – partly because I suspect that, whatever happens, quite a lot of the planet's organisms are going to get through, and that pleases me. I also think, with a bit of me, that we may actually come round and that a combination of human ingenuity and the growing awareness of the inbuilt wisdom of natural systems might actually just happen in the nick of time. I must say that I am some-what of James Lovelock's mind on this issue – that it may need a few more really bad catastrophes to nudge us into that position. It's terrible to say it, but the likely escalation of global climate disasters may actually be the one thing that pulls us up short, especially if they happen in Middle America rather than the poor southern states of America. But it may take that. It may take us to come to a point of true catastrophe before we sit up and realize what's happening.   **RICHARD MABEY**

it may take us to come to a point of true catastrophe before we sit up and realize what's happening

I honestly think things are going to get very bad. I think in the next 20, probably 30, years we're going to see accumulating suffering and dreadfulness as well – the whole Middle East and all the errors of that. So what we need is much more equity and international agreement, and we're breaking up what we've got. So in the short term, I'm very pessimistic. And I think the imbalances in the world economy will lead in some years to some kind of fairly big recession or depression. I hope I'm wrong, but I really think this is how it's going to be.

But I have enormous faith in just the human spirit and the goodness and decency and wisdom of most people in our country, ordinary people – not the elites, who I think are lost at the moment; they're not all monsters but they have lost their way – just ordinary folk and people in the developing world. And I think out of the growing mess will come – I hope, I think – a new wisdom, and we can create a new civilization that is just more equitable, and then we can live sustainably on the planet.

We could fail. It could just get nastier and nastier. We could have more and more war out of oil, water, access to food – corralling people who want to walk out of the poor places and come to where there is something. It could be very nasty indeed. We're going into very turbulent times.   **CLARE SHORT**

I don't have time to be optimistic, I don't have time to be pessimistic. All I know is that I see that there's a window of opportunity. There are some projects we're working on right now where we're trying to pull a lot of stakeholders together. We're trying to force a dialogue that gets people to think about these issues in a very big-picture way, in a very systematic way, and we'll see if it works. I'm doing this because I think I can, and I know it's the right thing to do, and that's what matters. If we succeed, great. But it's only because it needed to be done. It's only because we still had time to do it. If it's too late, well at least we tried. But we have to try. **CRAIG PACKER**

all I know is that I see that there's a window of opportunity

The dilemma for a lot of environmentalists is trying to get the balance right between the pessimistic interpretation of what's happening to the natural world and the need to be positive and optimistic to get more people to do more about it. They're sort of caught between Cassandra on the one hand and Pollyanna on the other hand.

And you can see that tension all the time in the environmental organizations. They don't want to come across as prophets of doom and gloom. They want to give people positive messages, but you can't do that in a false way. You've got to tell people what the reality is out there.

The problem is compounded by the fact that far too many people in the environment movement are really gloomy beggars, anyway. They don't cheer up very often, and they don't give themselves much of a chance to be as humorous as I think sometimes they ought to be. So that slightly downbeat, dowdy approach to the environment hasn't helped to engage more people, to get more people fired up with a sense of excitement about what it would look

that slightly downbeat, dowdy approach to the environment hasn't helped to engage more people, to get more people fired up with a sense of excitement about what it would look like to live responsible, environmentally friendly lifestyles

like to live responsible, environmentally friendly lifestyles. That would make such a difference. **JONATHON PORRITT**

It's very difficult to see how humans are on anything other than a one-way train. How do we significantly reduce our population numbers, how do we alter our critical dependence upon agriculturally produced resources, how do we reintroduce an appreciation of nature above and beyond the aesthetic, how do we reintroduce the notion that we simply borrow from the Earth?

I don't want to sound like a hippy now, but that is what hunter-gatherers do. How do we do all of this with people who view the world through their television screens, drink Coca-Cola and so on and so forth, you know? It is very difficult to be anything but pessimistic about this, and perhaps we have to appreciate that, certainly for the last 200 years, perhaps more, humans have really pulled themselves away from the general patterns of evolution of life on Earth. We have become something perhaps unique, if you like, a monster in that sense. It's very difficult to see how one can pull back from this. **PAUL PETITT**

I think where we've got it wrong is we've got the vision wrong. We've got wrong or at least incomplete the concept of what a positive future would look like. We haven't fleshed that out.

The environmental movement has been focused on the problems of save-the-whales and save-this and save-that, which were certainly real problems, but that doesn't motivate people in the long term; it doesn't provide them with a real focus and agenda for how to make things better. It's just how to keep things from getting worse, and I think that's where we've gone wrong.

And what we can do to get it right is to provide that vision, to create that vision, and that needs to be a shared vision. We've done some workshops where we actually got a group of very mixed people from very mixed backgrounds together and asked them to focus on that question and envision the world in the year 2100. What would you like to be there – for your children and grandchildren? Forget about where we are now or where we seem to be headed; how would you like it to be? And you get a lot of consensus on that issue in terms of the way people would really like the world to look.

I think we need to spend more time creating that positive vision, creating that shared vision and putting that picture out there as an alternative goal. If we want to get there, to that positive future, then what should we be doing now in order to achieve that goal as opposed to what we seem to be doing? And, in fact, most of our policy discussions are focused on small incremental changes – you know, right now, in the present, but leaving aside this broader picture and focusing on the future vision.   **ROBERT COSTANZA**

There are an awful lot of people now in the environment movement who think we're running out of time so fast that it may even be too late. There is a school of thought that says we've tripped the threshold on climate change and ecosystem degradation. I don't subscribe to that apocalyptic view – yet. I think there's still a window where the interventions we make will pull us back from that completely disastrous outcome for humankind. But it's not very big, and if we don't get on and make the changes that we need to make within the next five to ten years maximum, then I think those who, against their better nature, say it's too late will be proved right.

Oddly enough, I'm more optimistic today about the future than I was ten years ago, because I think that action follows awareness, and awareness is based on people understanding what's happening around them. And I watch these awareness curves, and I watch the way people are waking up to the stresses in the natural world, and I hear

> oddly enough, I'm more optimistic today about the future than I was ten years ago, because I think that action follows awareness, and awareness is based on people understanding what's happening around them

people saying, 'Well, perhaps we'd better do something about the environment after all' – something they'd never have said ten years ago. And what I know is happening is that enough of a body of potential support is opening up in electorates for politicians to begin to set some real leadership standards, so they can offer themselves to voters on a much greener ticket than they've ever done in the past. So I'm optimistic about that. Whether we've still got time to make that work, in terms of a big enough change in behaviour, I don't know the answer to that one. I suspect that we've got a lot less time than people think we have. But at least we are beginning now to see some serious political change coming in. **JONATHON PORRITT**

Yes I'm a great optimist, and I consider it a great misfortune that I should be given the job of presenting such a pessimistic prospect for our future, but it's not altogether pessimistic. The Earth is going to move into a very nasty state, and there won't be all that many survivors, but survivors there will be. We're a tough species.

Now, here on these islands – Great Britain I'm talking about – we will be faced with problems rather similar to those that happened a long time ago in the 1940s. In 1940 we were threatened by invasion from a very powerful force on the Continent. Many people gave up, threw up their arms in horror and said, 'There's nothing we can do. We'll just have to submit.' But we didn't submit, and times were not that bad. Many people who lived through them found them quite exciting and reward- ing, and many good things came from it. And I think exactly the same may happen as climate change comes to us here in the United Kingdom soon. It may seem a very selfish way of looking at things, looking after ourselves as a nation. It isn't, because we'd be no use to the world at all if we threw up our arms in horror and just sank. We have to survive in order to help those others in the world who will be in much greater need than we are. **JAMES LOVELOCK**

Well, you know it's very easy to get discouraged and throw up your hands and basically say we haven't been doing a very good job and let's just forget it. But you have to think about it as two sides of the ledger: the positive side, on which major conservation gains have taken place and the number of protected areas has multiplied many fold over 30 years; and there's the negative side. And the issue is not that there's nothing on the positive side – it's just that it's not enough.

Look at the Amazon, which is a place that I study at a lot. The Brazilian Amazon is now 40 per cent under protection. When I first went there, there was one national forest. That's an extraordinary achievement. The only problem is, if you really want to save the Amazon, you actually have to save the Amazon system, which makes half of its own rainfall. So you probably need something like 80 per cent in forest cover. And you know we're getting pretty close to that right now. So it's just a huge challenge.   **THOMAS LOVEJOY**

I find it very funny, as a religious person, to listen to the environmental movement telling me that the apocalypse is coming and we're all going to hell. I don't believe it. First and foremost, I think we're much more creative than we sometimes give ourselves credit. But I think the most important thing for me, and I say this as a Christian but also someone who works with all the major religions, is that ultimately the great faiths don't actually think that the whole purpose of creation is us at all. And there probably will come a time when there'll be no human beings, but there'll still be creation, and in the end the purpose of creation is not our existence.

We don't have to be here for creation to be appreciated. Every single faith says that creation is loved and held in the love of God. And God will still be here, and so will creation. So it can appear as though we're writing the longest kind of suicide note in history, but I don't think we are. I think as human beings we oscillate between apocalypse and Utopia. We oscillate between absolute despair and flagellating ourselves and then actually getting on and enjoying life.

And I see the environmental movement as essentially a missionary movement. It has a message. It believes that if we all do what it says and convert to its way of thinking the world will be saved. And like every missionary organization, it has to posit the opposite of that – we're going to hell. I actually think it's not true, and I think unless we have hope, and we really do have hope that things will change, nothing will. And the great faiths are all about taking people who felt that they were sinners, and lost and helpless, and saying, 'No you're not. You're loved, and you can become something other than you are.' So all the faiths believe that people can change and institutions can change. But also I think we just have to look at the fact that the world will go on. We may not be here, but I don't think that really matters.

I'm very challenged by the trilobite. The trilobite was probably the most successful species on Planet Earth. As a species it lasted for something like 250 million years, and then it died out. It's gone. Now what is the relevance of the trilobite to God or to humanity? It's a bit difficult to grapple with. But I think it raises fundamental questions. We assume that the worth of creation lies in our seeing it. But of course what the faiths say is, 'No. The worth of creation lies in the fact that God loves it.'

MARTIN PALMER

I don't honestly know whether the moral voice will be heard, if you ask me, practically speaking. I have a faith that it's worth trying, whatever happens – eminently worth trying. I also have some hope grounded on the fact that quite a lot of economists are now beginning to think again about how they assess profits, how they assess costs, and many of them are factoring in environmental costs to their economic projections as part of an overall balance sheet. I think that's one of the most significant changes in the world of economists recently, and I've been fascinated to see what's happening there. Unfortunately it takes time for all that to go forward, and time is not on our side in any of these things.

ROWAN WILLIAMS,
ARCHBISHOP OF CANTERBURY

> I also have … hope grounded on the fact that quite a lot of economists are now beginning to think again about how the costs, and many of them are factoring in environmental costs

I think the last message I'd like to leave from Tanzania is our common humanity. We're all people. Whether we're herding cattle or we're living in a palace somewhere – we're all people. And the same things that motivate us in the West motivate people out here, too. There's a certain level that we have to deal with, to get people to feel safe, to feel comfortable, to feel like this is in their best interests. We've decided, as societies, that enlightened self-interest is the best way forward. It's the best way forward for any kind of activity you engage in, and enlightened self-interest is the only hope. That means somebody is out here with nobody watching, with nobody telling him what to do, nobody trying to pound some message into his head. And it comes from within that – yes, this is something that we need to look after. That's the way to succeed.

We all have the same sense of community. In the right circumstances, that community requires us to look after our resources in the most fundamental way. We are all the same, and we all want this to be carefully protected, but only when we have clear self-interest in it. Our enlightenment is something that will come; it is something we can count on. It will be there, but we have to look after people's basic needs and protection before we can reach that point.   **CRAIG PACKER**

It seems to me that the issue of conservation of the natural world is something that can unite humanity, if the people know enough about it, and we can be persuaded to change the way in which we behave – that gross materialism and the search for material wealth are not the only things in life.   **DAVID ATTENBOROUGH**

We should think of our present problems as being the most singular opportunity for greatness that has ever been offered to any generation in any civilization in all of human history. If we fail to receive that opportunity, to act on it, then my feeling is we will become the most vilified generation that has ever lived in human history. However, if we act, we'll become heroes of whom our descendants will boast until the end of all history.   **ROGER PAYNE**

Biographies

Dr Neville Ash is Head of Ecosystem Assessment for the United Nations Environment Programme World Conservation Monitoring Centre (UNEP-WCMC), the biodiversity assessment and policy implementation arm of the United Nations Environment Programme. He has worked on various international assessments of the status of and trends in biodiversity and consequences of biodiversity change for people, and has previously done research and community work on the conservation of the Ethiopian wolf, Asian bear species and wildfowl.

Sir David Attenborough, world-famous broadcaster and television presenter, has worked in BBC television for more than 50 years, at one time as controller of BBC2. His epic series, seen worldwide, include *Life on Earth, Living Planet, The Trials of Life, Life of Mammals, Life of Birds, Life of Plants, Life in the Undergrowth, State of the Planet* and, more recently, *Planet Earth*, which he narrated. He has received countless awards, including Fellowship of the Royal Society, and many honorary degrees for his contributions to science and public awareness. He has been a Trustee of the British Museum, and the Royal Botanic Gardens, Kew, and President of the Royal Society for Nature Conservation.

Mark Brownlow is a Producer in the BBC Natural History Unit, who made the *Fresh Water* and the *Shallow Seas* programmes in the *Planet Earth* series. Other programmes he has produced include the award-winning *Smart Sharks – Swimming with Roboshark* and *Iguanas – Living like Dinosaurs*.

James Connaughton is the Chairman of the Council on Environmental Quality (CEQ) in the US. In this capacity, he serves as the Senior Environmental and Natural Resources Advisor to the President of the United States. He is also Director of the White House Office of Environmental Policy, which oversees the development of environmental policy, coordinates interagency implementation of environmental programmes, and mediates key policy disagreements among federal agencies, state, tribal and local governments and private citizens.

Huw Cordey is a Senior Producer in the BBC Natural History Unit, who made the *Deserts* and *Caves* programmes for the *Planet Earth* series. He was a producer for the series *Life of Mammals* and *Andes to Amazon*, and has produced a number of other films, including *Giant Otters – Wolves of the River* and *Space-age Reptiles*. He regularly contributes to Radio 4's *Nature* series.

Robert Costanza is Director of the Gund Institute for Ecological Economics at the University of Vermont, a transdisciplinary research and teaching institute that integrates natural and social science tools to address environmental research, policy and management issues at multiple scales, from small watersheds to global systems. Previously, he was Director of the University of Maryland's Institute for Ecological Economics and a professor in the Center for Environmental Science, at Solomons, and in the Biology Department at College Park. He is co-founder and past-president of the International Society for Ecological Economics, and was chief editor of the society's journal, *Ecological Economics*, from its inception until 2002. He currently serves on the editorial board of eight other international academic journals and is

President of the International Society for Ecosystem Health. He is the author or co-author of more than 300 scientific papers, and his work has been cited in more than 3000 scientific articles.

Ahmed Djoghlaf, who holds the rank of Assistant Secretary General of the United Nations, has been Executive Secretary of the United Nations Convention on Biological Diversity since January 2006. Previously, he served for two and a half years as Assistant Executive Director of UNEP, the United Nations Environment Programme, while maintaining his responsibilities as Director and Coordinator of UNEP's Division of the Global Environment Facility (GEF). During the seven years he was at the helm of the GEF, the portfolio grew from 6 projects worth $28 million to 600 projects worth more than $1 billion, implemented in 155 countries. A diplomat by training, he has served as a Special Adviser on Environment to the Prime Minister of Algeria and Special Adviser to three Algerian Ministers of Foreign Affairs. He went on to serve as General Rapporteur of the Preparatory Committee of the 1992 United Nations Conference on Environment and Development, Special Adviser to the Executive Secretary of the Convention on Biological Diversity and a Vice Chairman of the Negotiating Committee on the Framework Convention on Climate Change and the Convention to Combat Desertification. Mr Djoghlaf holds five post-university degrees, including a PhD in Political Sciences from the University of Nancy, France.

Dr James A. Duke is one of the world's leading medicinal-plant scientists. He worked for 30 years as a botanist with the United States Department of Agriculture (USDA) and is the author of a number of classic books on medicinal plants, including the best-selling *The Green Pharmacy*, on the use of plants to treat some 100 diseases or disorders.

Johan Eliasch bought a 160,000-hectare (400,000-acre) plot – the size of Greater London – in the heart of the Amazon rainforest in Brazil from a logging company to protect the habitat. He is Chairman of the Management Board of Head NV and Group Chief Executive Officer, and Chairman of Equity Partners Limited and of London Films. Mr Eliasch has also served as a Special Adviser to the Shadow Foreign Secretary and is the Deputy Party Treasurer of the Conservative party. He is a member of a number of advisory boards.

Alastair Fothergill is the Series Producer of *Planet Earth* and the Director of *Earth*, the associated feature film. He joined the BBC Natural History Unit (NHU) in 1983, working on many series, including *The Really Wild Show*, *Wildlife on One* and *The Trials of Life*. He was appointed head of the NHU in 1992, and during his tenure he produced the award-winning Antarctic series *Life in the Freezer*. After stepping down as head, he went on to produce another award-winning series, *The Blue Planet*. He has presented a number of tv programmes, including *The Abyss*, and is the author of three books.

John Hare is the founder of the Wild Camel Protection Foundation, which he set up in 1997 to protect the critically endangered wild Bactrian camel in the Gobi and Gashun Gobi Deserts in northwest China and southwest Mongolia. He is a Fellow of the Royal Geographical Society and the Explorers' Club of America, and has made seven expeditions to the desert habitat of the wild Bactrian camel. He has been awarded the Ness Award by the Royal Geographical Society for wild Bactrian camel conservation, the Lawrence of Arabia medal for exploration under hazard by the Royal Society for Asian Affairs and the Mungo Park Medal for exploration by the Royal Scottish Geographical Society.

Dr Chadden Hunter is a world expert on gelada baboons, which he has studied in the Simien highlands of Ethiopia for more than seven years. His previous research includes the courtship behaviour of bowerbirds in Australia, and he has been a scientific consultant for a number of BBC programmes including *Wild Africa*, *Life of Mammals*, *Nile* and *Planet Earth*, and has appeared in many others, including National Geographic's *Cliffhangers*.

Tony Juniper is the Vice-Chair of Friends of the Earth International and Executive Director of Friends of the Earth England, Wales and Northern Ireland, and a leading broadcaster and commentator on environmental matters. He plays a frontline role in many FoE campaigns and has a particular interest in policy questions linked to the activities of transnational corporations. A member of the World Parrot Trust's Scientific Committee, he is author of *Spix's Macaw: The Race to Save the World's Rarest Bird* and co-author of the award-winning *Parrots of the World*.

Jan Kees Vis is Sustainable Agriculture Director of Unilever (Foods), supporting the 11 lead programmes around the world putting the principles of sustainable agriculture into practice. He chairs the executive board of the Roundtable on Sustainable Palm Oil, comprising growers, processors, consumer-goods manufacturers, retailers, investors and NGOs working towards ensuring a sustainable supply of palm oil.

Peyton Knight is Director of Environmental and Regulatory Affairs for the National Center for Public Policy Research, a US communications and research foundation supportive of a strong national defence and dedicated to providing free-market solutions to today's public policy problems. Firm in the belief that private owners are the best stewards of the environment, the NCPPR advocates private, free-market solutions to environmental challenges. Mr Knight is a graduate of the College of William and Mary, where he concentrated his studies on public policy. He has testified several times before both Houses of the US Congress and has been quoted in numerous print media outlets across the US. He is also a frequent guest on many radio and TV programmes, including the Fox News Channel, CNN, the BBC and MSNBC.

James P. Leape is the Director General of WWF International. He has worked in nature conservation for more than 25 years, beginning his career as an environmental lawyer in the US, and advising the United Nations Environment Programme (UNEP). For 10 years, he directed the worldwide conservation programmes of WWF-US, serving as Executive Vice-President, and for four years, he directed the conservation and science initiatives of the David and Lucile Packard Foundation, one of the largest conservation funders in the world.

Dr Thomas Lovejoy, a distinguished tropical and conservation biologist, is currently President of the Heinz Center in the US. He is generally credited with having brought the issue of tropical deforestaton to the fore as a public issue and was the first person to use the term biological diversity (in 1980), and in the same year, made the first projection of global extinction rates in the Global 2000 Report to the President. He is also the originator of the concept of debt-for-nature swaps, and the founder of the public-television series *Nature*. Dr Lovejoy has served as Executive Vice-President of WWF-US, Assistant Secretary for Environmental and External Affairs for the Smithsonian Institution, Counselor to the Secretary for Biodiversity and Environmental Affairs and Chief Biodiversity Advisor for the World Bank. He is past President of the American Institute of Biological Sciences, past Chairman of the United States Man and Biosphere Program, and past President of the Society for Conservation Biology.

Dr James Lovelock is one of the most distinguished and controversial commentators in the UK on environmental issues, best known for originating the Gaia hypothesis (subject of his 1979 book *Gaia: A New Look at Life on Earth*), which considers Earth as a self-regulating living system. He has a PhD. in medicine and a DSc in biophysics, and worked at the National Institute for Medical Research in London. Later he collaborated on lunar and planetary research with NASA's Jet Propulsion Laboratory. His interdisciplinary research covers such broad fields as medicine, biology, geophysiology, and instrument science. He has filed more than 50 patents for his inventions, one of which, the electron-capture detector, first revealed the ubiquitous distribution of pesticide residues, PCBs, nitrous oxide and the CFCs responsible for atmospheric ozone depletion. His latest book is *The Revenge of Gaia*.

Dr Barbara Maas is Chief Executive of Care for the Wild International, a conservation and animal-welfare charity that protects wildlife against cruelty and exploitation. A zoologist by training, she studied the behaviour of Serengeti bat-eared foxes at the University of Cambridge and rabies in endangered canids at Oxford University. She has been a scientific adviser to numerous conservation and animal-welfare organisations and worked in marine conservation in the New Zealand civil service. Her twin passions are understanding and helping animals.

Professor Wangari Muta Maathai is a Member of Parliament for the Tetu Constituency and Kenya's Assistant Minister for the Environment. She was the creator of the Green Belt Movement, a broad-based, grass-roots organization, the main focus of which is empowering women's groups to plant trees to conserve the environment and improve quality of life. She was the first woman in East and Central Africa to earn a doctoral degree (in biological sciences) and went on to become Chair of the Department of Veterinary Anatomy at the University of Nairobi. Professor Maathai has served on the UN Commission for Global Governance and the Commission on the Future, and she and the Green Belt Movement have received numerous awards, most notably the 2004 Nobel Peace Prize. She serves on the boards of several organizations, including the UN Secretary General's Advisory Board on Disarmament, the Women's Environment and Development Organization (WEDO), World Learning (USA), Green Cross International, Environment Liaison Centre International, the WorldWIDE Network of Women in Environmental Work and the National Council of Women of Kenya.

Richard Mabey is one of Britain's foremost writers and a leading commentator on nature and our relationship with it. His seminal books include *The Unofficial Countryside, Common Ground, Food for Free, Flora Britannica* – winner of several major book awards – and, most recently, *Nature Cure*. His biography of Gilbert White won the Whitbread Biography Award, and his thought-provoking essays are widely published in magazines and newspapers in the UK.

Dr Jeffrey A. McNeely is Chief Scientist for the IUCN – The World Conservation Union, responsible for overseeing all of IUCN's scientific work. Trained as an anthropologist and zoologist, he spent 12 years in Asia advising on conservation issues in Thailand, Indonesia, Nepal, Laos, Cambodia, and Vietnam. He has published more than 400 technical and popular articles on a wide range of conservation issues, seeking to link conservation of natural resources to the maintenance of cultural diversity and to economically sustainable ways of life. He is one of the most respected researchers and writers on biodiversity and its importance.

Nisar Malik is the Chief Executive of Walkabout Films, a conservationist and an extreme-events organizer based in Pakistan, who helped the *Planet Earth* team achieve remarkable shots of wild snow leopards. He worked with ITN as a Field Producer covering Afghanistan and Pakistan from 1989 to 2002 and has made documentaries and organized extreme events in the Hindukush, Karakorams and Himalayas. His intimate knowledge of the area meant that, after the devastating earthquake of 2005, he was able to set up the 'Quake Jumpers' – mobile teams of mountain experts able to reach communities in the Himalayas that other aid workers were unable to. As a UN World Food Programme Emergency Field Advisor, he also assisted in setting up of the largest peacetime helicopter operation in the history of the UN to reach quake victims. Nisar is currently making a programme with the BBC on the wildlife of the remote north of Pakistan.

Dr Tony Martin began his research on Amazon river dolphins, or botos, with the Natural Environment Research Council in Cambridge, and continues it through St Andrew's University. His time in the tropics has always competed with a passion for polar regions, north and south. He now studies whales, seals and petrels for the British Antarctic Survey around the island of South Georgia, which was the centre of the global whaling industry at its peak and where, to his joy, whales are emerging from the abyss and appearing in greater numbers each year.

Robert, Lord May of Oxford, was President of the Royal Society (2000-2005) and holds a Professorship jointly in the Department of Zoology, Oxford University, and at Imperial College, London, and is a Fellow of Merton College, Oxford. For the five-year period ending September 2000, he was Chief Scientific Adviser to the UK Government and Head of its Office of Science and Technology. His current research deals with factors influencing the diversity and abundance of plant and animal species, and with the rates, causes and consequences of extinction. He was awarded a Knighthood in 1996 and appointed a Companion of the Order of Australia in 1998, both for 'services to science'. In 2002, the Queen appointed him to the Order of Merit. Lord May is a member of the US National Academy of Sciences and an honorary life member or fellow of various other learned societies. He holds honorary degrees from more than 20 universities worldwide.

Dr Russell A. Mittermeier is President of Conservation International (CI) and a prominent primatologist, herpetologist and wildlife conservationist, with more than 35 years of field experience in Central and South America, Africa and Asia. His areas of expertise include biological diversity and its value to humanity, ecosystem conservation, tropical biology and species conservation. Dr Mittermeier's publications include 15 books and more than 400 papers and popular articles on primates, reptiles, tropical forests and biodiversity. Dr Mittermeier has served as Chairman of the IUCN Species Survival Commission's Primate Specialist Group since 1977, been an Adjunct Professor at the State University of New York at Stony Brook since 1978, and President of the Margot Marsh Biodiversity Foundation since 1996. Prior to working for CI, he was with WWF-US for 11 years, where his last role was Vice-President for Science. He is a recipient of the San Diego Zoo's Gold Medal, the Order of the Golden Ark from His Royal Highness Prince Bernhard of the Netherlands, the Grand National Order of the Southern Cross from the Government of Brazil and the Grand Sash and Order of the Yellow Star from the Government of the Republic of Suriname. In 1998, he was named one of *Time Magazine*'s 'Heroes for the Planet'.

Dr Craig Packer is Distinguished McKnight Professor in the Department of Ecology, Evolution & Behavior at the University of Minnesota and a world expert on lions. He has studied baboons in Tanzania with Jane Goodall and Japanese macaques, and since 1978, he has headed up the Serengeti lion project in Tanzania. He is also the principal investigator of collaborative research projects in the Serengeti. His book *Into Africa* won the 1995 John Burroughs Medal, and he has written 83 scientific articles, 55 of which concern his research on lions.

Martin Palmer is the Secretary General of the Alliance for Religions and Conservation, founded in 1995 by HRH Prince Philip, a secular body that helps the major religions of the world develop their own environmental programmes, based on their own core teachings, beliefs and practices and creates powerful alliances between faith communities and conservation groups. A theologian and Chinese scholar, he is a frequent TV and radio broadcaster and the author of numerous books on the spiritual traditions of East and West. Religious adviser to WWF and to a range of other development and environmental groups, he also advises communities within 11 different major faiths on their practical and philosophical relationships with nature.

Dr Roger Payne is one of the world's leading whale biologists. He is best known for his discovery (with Scott McVay) that humpback whales sing songs and for proving that the sounds of fin and blue whales can be heard across oceans. He has studied the behaviour of whales since 1967 and is founder and President of the Ocean Alliance. He has led more than 100 expeditions to all oceans and studied every species of large whale in the wild. A pioneer of many of the benign research techniques now used throughout the world to study free-swimming whales, he has trained many of the current leaders in whale research, both in North America and abroad. He has founded long-term research projects on the songs of humpbacks and on the behaviour of 1300 individually known Argentine right whales – the longest continuous study of its kind. His institute's research vessel has recently finished collecting biopsies from 960 sperm whales, on a five-year round-the-world voyage, which will show the true degree to which the seas are now contaminated.

Dr Paul Pettitt is a Senior Lecturer in Palaeolithic Archaeology at the University of Sheffield. He is an expert on the European Middle and Upper Palaeolithic and the African Middle Stone Age, in particular the Neanderthals and their lifestyle and the likely affect of climate change on their survival, and has published more than 100 scientific papers. From 1995 to 2002, he was Senior Archaeologist in the Radiocarbon Accelerator Unit at Oxford University, during which time he was Douglas Price Junior Research Fellow at Keble College and Research Fellow and Tutor in Archaeology and Anthropology at Keble College. He has worked on numerous television and radio programmes, including *Horizon*, *Walking with Beasts*, and *Walking with Cavemen*, and was scientific consultant for Channel Four's *Neanderthal* and *Ice World*.

Jonathon Porritt is a leading writer, broadcaster and commentator on sustainable development and is co-founder and Programme Director of Forum for the Future – the UK's chief sustainable development charity. He is also Chairman of the UK Sustainable Development Commission (SDC), the Government's principal source of independent advice across the whole sustainable development agenda, is a member of the Board of the South West Regional Development Agency, co-Director of the Prince of Wales's Business and Environment Programme and Vice-President of the Socialist Environment Resource Association (SERA). He was a former Director of Friends of the Earth and co-Chair of the Green Party, of which he is still a member. He has written a number of influential books, including *Capitalism As If the World Matters*.

Sandra Postel is a leading authority on international freshwater issues and author of three highly acclaimed books on the subject. She is founder and Director of the Global Water Policy Project in the US, which promotes the preservation and sustainable use of Earth's fresh water through research, writing, consulting and public speaking. She is also Visiting Senior Lecturer in Environmental Studies at Mount Holyoke College. From 1988 until 1994, she served as Vice President for Research at the Worldwatch Institute, a non-profit research organization, with which she remains affiliated as Senior Fellow. In 2002, she was named one of the 'Scientific American 50' by *Scientific American* magazine, an award recognizing contributions to science and technology.

Adam Ravetch is one of only a handful of Arctic film-makers who shoot under the ice. His 15 years' filming in the north has enabled him to become an award-winning cinematographer working for the top wildlife companies in the industry, as well as producing seven Arctic films of his own for National Geographic and PBS.

Dr M. Sanjayan is a Lead Scientist for the Nature Conservancy, a leading US-based conservation organization working to protect the most ecologically important lands and waters around the world for nature and people. He has also recently developed and launched the Nature Conservancy's new Africa Program. He has served as a consultant to the World Bank and Global Environmental Facility on conservation and development projects and on conservation area designs/planning for many smaller conservation organizations. His most recent publication is the co-edited book *Connectivity Conservation*. He also holds a faculty appointment in the Wildlife Program at the University of Montana, in Missoula.

Clare Short MP was, until May 2003, Secretary of State for International Development (DFID) – a new ministry created after the 1997 general election to promote policies for sustainable development and the elimination of poverty, which manages Britain's programme of assistance to developing countries. She has worked as a civil servant at the Home Office, as a Director of Youthaid and the Unemployment Unit and as a Director of AFFOR, a community-based organization promoting racial equality in Birmingham.

Peter Smith, Roman Catholic Archbishop of Cardiff, is Chairman of the Department of Christian Responsibility and Citizenship of the Catholic Bishops' Conference of England & Wales and Chairman of the Catholic Truth Society. He was Bishop of East Anglia for 10 years and Chairman of the Central Religious Advisory Committee of the BBC and ITC from 2001 to 2004, and is a Fellow of Cardiff University and an Honorary Fellow of the University of Wales, Lampeter.

Dr Mark Stanley Price, Chief Executive of the Durrell Wildlife Conservation Trust, was the founder-chair of the World Conservation Union's (IUCN) Reintroduction Specialist Group. He devised what is universally recognized as the model approach to reintroducing species, based on his experience in the 1980s of reintroducing captive-bred white (Arabian) oryx back into the wild in Oman and is a commentator on conservation issues worldwide. For 12 years from 1987, Dr Stanley Price worked as Director of African Operations with the African Wildlife Foundation (AWF), in Kenya, developing the organization as an effective force in African conservation. From 1998 to 2001, he sat on the Board of Trustees for the Kenya Wildlife Service.

Dr Robert T. Watson is Chief Scientist at the World Bank in the Sustainable Development Network. He has worked on environmental issues since the 1980s (including ozone depletion, global warming and biodiversity) and was the Chair of the Intergovernmental Panel on Climate Change between 1996 and 2002 and Board co-Chair of the recently published Millennium Ecosystem Assessment. Dr Watson had previously been Director for Environment at the World Bank, served in the White House Office of Science and Technology Policy under President Bill Clinton, and worked at NASA. He has received many national and international awards and prizes for his contributions to science, including an Honorary Companion of the Order of Saint Michael and Saint George from the UK, and the American Association for the Advancement of Sciences Award for Scientific Freedom and Responsibility, as well as eight awards from NASA for distinguished service over the years. He is also a member of UNEP's Global 500: The Roll of Honour for Environmental Achievement.

Dr Rowan Williams, Archbishop of Canterbury is Primate of all England – the nation's senior Christian and spiritual voice and leader of the Anglican communion (about 70 million members throughout the world). Rowan Williams is also a distinguished academic. He was Professor of Theology at the University of Oxford, has written a number of books on the history of theology and spirituality, including two books of poetry, and is a Fellow of the British Academy.

Professor E.O. Wilson is one of the world's most distinguished biologists and thinkers and a passionate naturalist. Currently Pellegrino University Professor Emeritus and Honorary Curator in Entomology at Harvard University, he is also the world's leading expert on ants. The recipient of many scientific and conservation honours, including two Pulitzer Prizes, he was named by *Time Magazine* as one of the 25 most influential people in the US. He is also a leading modern-science writer. Classic books he has written include the controversial *Sociobiology: The New Synthesis*, a work that advanced evolutionary thinking, *On Human Nature*, *The Diversity of Life*, *The Biophilia Hypothesis* and *Consilience: The Unity of Knowledge*.

Index

Also available

This is the major book-of-the-series *Planet Earth*. Written by the producers of the series and Illustrated with more than 400 remarkable photographs of the world's most extraordinary wildlife and natural features, it is a permanent record of one of the most ambitious natural history projects every undertaken for television.

Planet Earth – The Making of an Epic Series goes behind the scenes with the production teams, recounting tales of discovery, drama and hair-raising exploits. Packed with fascinating interviews with the film-makers and more than 100 unique production photographs, it also provides an insight into the ingenious techniques used to produce the ground-breaking series.